To Laurel,

WOOF

WHY ORDINARY ORGANIZATIONS FAIL

Lori
Turner-Wilson

WOOF - WHY ORDINARY ORGANIZATIONS FAIL

My sincere gratitude to Donna Collier, Michelle Cunningham, Carl Cottam, Ashley McHugh, and Tammie Ritchey for their contributions to this book. Without you, WOOF would still be but an idea.

A special thanks to Julie Lunn – my partner in crime and RedRover co-founder – who had the courage to take the leap with me. It's been a doggone incredible ride from start-up to where we are today. I can't imagine taking this journey with anyone else, and your friendship has meant the world.

And thank you to the entire RedRover team that serves as daily inspiration to our clients and to me personally.

Photography by Steve Jones © www.stevejonesphoto.com.

ISBN #978193694672-3
First Edition

© Copyright 2016 by The Nautilus Publishing Company
426 South Lamar Blvd., Suite 16
Oxford, MS 38655, Tel: 662-513-0159
www.nautiluspublishing.com

PRINTED IN CANADA
through a partnership with Friesnes Printing, Louisville, Kentucky

WOOF is dedicated to my father, the late Chuck Turner, who taught us the value of relationships and the true responsibility of a sales professional; to my inspirational mother, Rita Turner, who always let us know anything was possible; and to my ever-supportive husband, Mike Wilson, for his humor and endless patience through all of the late nights and weekends necessary to build a business.

TABLE OF CONTENTS

CHAPTER ONE
ESTABLISH A STRATEGY

CHAPTER TWO
EXECUTE YOUR MARKETING STRATEGY

CHAPTER THREE
EXECUTE YOUR SALES STRATEGY

CHAPTER FOUR
MEASURE YOUR SALES & MARKETING STRATEGIES

WOOF is an accumulation of the sales and marketing lessons I've learned throughout my life, starting at an age earlier than most. I was raised by a salesman for a father, and that upbringing gave me a unique perspective on the world. It helped me understand that relationships and integrity are at the core of all business. It gave me an appreciation for the responsibility that a true sales professional carries – listening, understanding, empathizing and partnering. In my view, there are few professions as challenging or noble.

My first attempt at applying the skills which I saw my father demonstrate in his work and life came when I was just seven years old. I planned, promoted and executed an event – a dog show, in fact. The show was widely attended by children throughout the neighborhood, received rave reviews, and even earned a profit. It was, on the surface, a silly childhood game. But it began to shape who I was meant to be.

Sales degrees weren't common in the late eighties when I entered college, so marketing was my path. I first attended the University of Arkansas and then moved on to the University of Nebraska to complete my degree. Shortly after college, I ventured into the corporate world, ultimately leading marketing, sales and communications teams for top national and international companies including Hampton Hotels, TCBY Enterprises and First Horizon National Corporation. While my education and much of my early training were in marketing, I've always looked at marketing through a sales lens.

My corporate roles afforded me the opportunity to partner with some of the most well-known advertising agencies in the world. Through those experiences, some outstanding and others less than ideal, I could visualize the type of agency I would someday build – one where sales and marketing strategies align; plans are grounded in comprehensive, meaningful research; teams begin with the end in mind, keenly focused on tangible metrics; and campaigns are launched to achieve bottom-line impact, not just to add to a library of colorful or clever creative.

This vision is the foundation of RedRover Sales & Marketing Strategy, a company I co-founded with Julie Lunn ten years ago in Memphis, Tennessee.

For more than five years, I've had the honor of writing a syndicated column, called "Guerrilla Sales & Marketing," for daily and weekly papers across the Southeast. WOOF is a collection of the most transformative of those columns. My hope is for the book to help you achieve your organization's transformation.

1

Just as a heart surgeon would never cut before a diagnosis, so should go your sales and marketing strategy. A proper diagnosis requires objective, comprehensive research insights that can only be gathered by gaining the authentic perspectives of your current customers and the broader marketplace. Only through proper research can you determine the sales and marketing levers to pull in order to generate a strong, predictable return on investment.

ESTABLISH A STRATEGY

WHAT TO DO WHEN YOU'RE NOT STEVE JOBS

SEVENTY PERCENT of startup businesses fail within the first 10 years, according to a 2013 study conducted by Bradley University and the University of Tennessee. It's a devastating reality, especially since most of those startups are small businesses, which generate more than half of domestic sales in the U.S.

More often than not, these failures are caused by a lack of solid management abilities. Ironically, the very qualities that inspire most entrepreneurs to take a risk and start a new business can work against them when it comes to actually leading that business day-to-day, because there are inherent differences between entrepreneurs and leaders.

Entrepreneurs are visionaries and innovators, but they may tire when it comes to execution. Entrepreneurs tend to favor the newest strategy instead of a tried-and-true strategy, since they are more comfortable with risk. While they don't enjoy executing day-to-day tasks, they may struggle in effectively delegating those responsibilities to others as well.

Leaders consistently execute company strategy. They appreciate both the need to hire seasoned managers and the benefits of empowering them to make decisions autonomously. Often, however, leaders lack the entrepreneurial trait of being able to inspire a workforce to drive toward a greater vision, and they may struggle to maintain a culture of innovation.

An entrepreneurial leader is a rare bird. These are the people who inspire us with both their vision and ability to see it through, like Steve Jobs, Sam Walton, Henry Ford and Bill Gates. However, it typically takes a strong, balanced partnership between an entrepreneur and a leader for a startup business to find success.

If a management imbalance occurs, a sales and marketing strategy is not likely to produce a strong return on your investment. If an entrepreneur is solely at the helm, seemingly continuous changes in sales and marketing direction can result in team confusion and spinning of wheels without solid results. When a leader is alone in the driver's seat, the business may become stagnant, focused too much on the strategies of the past without an eye to future innovation. Neither environment is suitable for sustainable growth.

Too many businesses fail simply due to a lack of balance between entrepreneurial innovation and leadership. To ensure your business thrives, recognize your natural strengths and truly empower trusted business partners to balance out your management team.

Combining entrepreneurial qualities with steady leadership is the key to long-term success.

DIFFERENCE BETWEEN A RUT AND A GRAVE

THROUGH THE YEARS, I've come to embrace the realization that I am an agent of change for companies dissatisfied with their current sales and marketing outcomes. Once, after I proposed some significant strategy changes to an area CEO, I was startled when he told me, with perfect clarity, "We can't expect a different outcome if we aren't willing to change what we're doing."

We can all surely agree that this statement holds true. Why, then, do so many businesses struggle in executing change? Most business owners and managers will say they embrace change, but do their actions align with their words?

There have been many studies over the years about the psychology of change, our natural resistance to it and how we can better navigate through it. Embracing change, when it is foreign to you, is like breaking a bad habit of routine complacency.

Dr. Dawn Obrecht, an addiction specialist, describes three ingredients needed to bring about real change: honesty, openness and willingness. How open are you to hearing about the need for change? How honest are you being with yourself and others about your desire and willingness to change?

Willingness to change is best measured by action. If you're willing to stop talking about change and actually take action, regardless of your comfort level in doing so, that's half the battle.

If you're not pleased with your current sales and marketing outcomes, how do you assess which elements of your strategy should change?

Talk with customers and prospects. Ask what they see as your differentiators, what would make them more likely to buy, what product/service enhancements they desire, and what your competitors are doing well. Then shop those competitors just like a customer would. How do your efforts stack up?

Shadow your sales reps, identifying any missed opportunities or skill gaps. And assess the return on your past sales and marketing strategies. If your efforts can't be measured, work to find strategies that can be.

If you know you are simply too close to the situation to objectively assess it or too uncomfortable to drive real change, simply find someone more removed who can. It is the best gift you can give your company.

Pulitzer-prize-winning novelist Ellen Glasgow summed it up well when she said, "The only difference between a rut and a grave is their dimensions." Don't let complacency kill your business. Be an agent of change.

REWIRING YOUR INHERENT RESISTANCE TO CHANGE

WHY DO SO MANY great organizations struggle with change? After all, as the Greek philosopher Heraclitus once said, "the only thing that is constant is change," and that sentiment couldn't be truer today.

Steve McKee got to the heart of the challenge in his book *"When Growth Stalls."* In the book, he studied over 5,000 companies, only to find that 41.2 percent of them stalled notably in the last decade.

McKee identified several interrelated reasons for these corporate stalls, but two of the most important reasons were that the company had no point of differentiation from their competitors, and that the company was unable to adjust to new market realities.

Many businesses begin with a point of differentiation but if they fail to adjust quickly enough to changing markets, that point of differentiation can simply be lost to a more nimble, adaptable competitor.

What causes that failure to adjust to change? Cultural anthropologist, Andrea Simon, in a 2013 Forbes article titled "Why We're So Afraid of Change — and Why That Holds Businesses Back," said it boils down to these three realities.

Habits are powerful. Our brain limits what it sees over time, and our current reality essentially conforms to past perceptions — or what we know. Those early experiences prevent us from seeing things in new, innovative ways unless we push ourselves to do so.

Our brains hate change. As we learn something new, our prefrontal cortex is working in overdrive, and it is exhausting. That's why our natural tendency is to stick with what we know versus pushing the proverbial boulder uphill.

You have to experience new ways of doing things to really accept change, instead of just reading or talking about it. However, to do something new, you must actually allow the change to begin in the first place, despite any possible anxiety. While due diligence is important when considering changes to implement, avoid getting so caught up in analysis — which can often be a stall tactic in disguise — that your change efforts fizzle out.

It may help you to move forward if you remember that change doesn't have to be permanent. Just make sure you are measuring the results of the change and adapting your strategy quickly as you go.

Even though creating change can be challenging, it is essential that your business continues to adapt to evolving consumer and market demands, so that your company doesn't end up stalled like so many others. If you are aware of your inherent resistance to change, you are more apt to battle through that natural internal wiring and persevere at continuously improving and preparing your company for future market realities.

And that's the kind of company-wide mark every business professional wants to leave.

BEWARE OF SHINY OBJECTS

THE VERY QUALITY that defines some of the world's greatest entrepreneurs is the downfall of many. How's that for irony?

The Harvard Business Review reports that most serial entrepreneurs display several common traits: persuasion, leadership, personal accountability, interpersonal skills and goal-orientation. Likewise, there are several vital skills, necessary for long-term success, that many entrepreneurs lack. One of the main missing skills is the ability to stick with a plan.

Entrepreneurs are practically defined by their desire to continuously improve, whether that means improving products, processes, sales strategies or a marketing approach. As serial innovators, most entrepreneurs thrive on change, even though the majority of the population is wired to avoid change. This desire to innovate and evolve strategies can certainly work to the entrepreneur's benefit. But the desire for change, unchecked, can result in Shiny Object Syndrome if you're not careful: the desire for change for the sake of change alone.

You might be suffering from Shiny Object Syndrome:

If you're itching to veer from the course only a month or two after implementing a carefully considered 12-month plan.

If you are always one of the first to invest time in the latest, trendiest social media channel even before there are enough participants for that effort to be worth your while.

If you will easily abandon proven strategies that generate a positive, measurable return in favor of new ideas that might have a chance to do better.

If you are known for executing one-time marketing strategies — a sponsorship here, an advertisement there — but not with enough frequency for the market to remember you.

If your staff feels like all of your directional changes keep them from completing projects.

If you've just diagnosed yourself with Shiny Object Syndrome, don't despair. Awareness is the first step in the path to improvement.

Begin by surrounding yourself with a management team or advisors with planning skills and a sense of determination. You should remain an active participant in the development of your company's sales and marketing plan, but trust your team to thoroughly evaluate the ideas you generate with your innate creativity. Make sure that you agree with your team about how to determine a specific, measurable definition of success.

However, once you've signed off on the plan they've crafted, step out of the way and allow your team to follow through unfettered. If your team is achieving goals, give everyone a pat on the back for sticking to the plan, and then allow them to continue without interference. By empowering and placing your trust in your team — and in the strategy you have worked together to create — you will see greater results.

MARKETING ON A WING AND A PRAYER

THE AVERAGE COMPANY spends 3 to 5 percent of revenue on marketing, which is certainly not a trivial expense. Why, then, do so many companies invest so little time in the construction of the marketing plans that ensure their investments are getting results?

Remember that your organization's steady growth is dependent upon the strength of your marketing plan, and bid farewell to wishful marketing plans that ride on a wing and a prayer. Instead, use research to guide the creation of an informed plan that will generate a predictable return on your investment.

There are two reasons that you should begin building your marketing plan by conducting research. No business owner can be entirely objective about the current situation of his company and the competitive landscape, as well as the honest perceptions and needs of customers and prospects. Research can help you gain the objectivity of an outsider. Research can also help you come to new revelations about your market, industry or customer base. After all, you don't know what you don't know — until you engage in market research.

Begin with qualitative research, which is necessary to ensure you fully understand the broad scope of the opportunities for growth, as well as the various obstacles you will face in executing your plan. Qualitative research is subjective in nature and often takes the form of focus groups or interviews with a small sampling of internal or external stakeholders. For example, your internal stakeholders might be your employees, your management or your board of directors. Customers, prospects and influencers would all be considered external stakeholders. You should also incorporate a competitive assessment into your qualitative research by shopping competitors and evaluating their public communications and marketing efforts.

With this new information in hand, you are ready to validate those findings through quantitative, numerical research. Quantitative research is more objective in nature and is based on hard data, often featuring fixed-response options like you would find in a survey. Be sure to survey a large enough number of people, so that you can be confident your findings are accurate. If you skip this step, you risk making major marketing decisions based on small-scale findings that may not be representative of your market.

A high-level financial assessment and marketing audit can also provide valuable insights. When you are conducting the financial assessment, examine your profit margins by product and service line, taking into consideration internal capacity for growth, so that you are crystal clear on where best to apply your marketing dollars. With the marketing audit, pull analytics available from your website, email campaigns and social media efforts, at a minimum, from the prior year.

Research, if properly executed, will inevitably bring to light the most efficient plan to grow your organization.

CAN PASSION BECOME POISON?

THE ROMAN SCHOLAR Marcus Tullius Cicero saw the stifling danger of too much passion more than 2,000 years ago when he wrote, "He only employs his passion who can make no use of his reason." When you're passionate about your business, it can be downright difficult to be objective, which can severely limit your company's growth.

Take, for example, Company X.

Company X has been in business for 30 years. The firm's principal and founder built a strong, loyal client base. The clients share a similar demographic and psychographic make-up as the founder. They are in the same age range, share the same conservative beliefs and appreciate the firm's "old school" ways. The founder is convinced the business model she developed has served the company very well through the years.

The challenge is that the client base is aging, and younger generations are either not aware of the firm or find the brand to be irrelevant — from the out-of-date service model, to the dated brand image, to the firm's lack of an online presence. Because of all of this, Company X is virtually invisible to the younger generation of clients.

While the founder is sincerely interested in attracting a new client base, it's difficult for her to be objective about the right strategies. Why? These new strategies just don't appeal to her. After all, she built this highly successful company trusting her gut instincts. While those instincts have been good at bringing in like-minded clients, her instincts are now limiting her ability to attract new consumers.

She loves this business that she spent her life building — so much so that fear is preventing her from moving the company forward by trying something new.

What's the answer? Having an objective third-party research firm talk to prospective customers from the younger, targeted demographic can help the founder understand how these customers perceive the brand today, what they would like to see updated to help them better connect, and how and when they want to hear from the company. Research can provide proof that your preferences may not match those of your target audience.

If she still isn't convinced, she can confirm what she learned from the research with some market testing, often called A-B testing. Her marketing team can deliver two different email campaigns, for example, at the same time to similar younger audiences — one with a more modernized messaging strategy and one using her tried-and-true tone. Measuring the responses to each may set her mind at ease that change will have a desired effect. If her loyal clients are truly loyal, a more modern brand won't stop them from coming back, but she will also be opening the doors to a whole new customer.

If you want to create a legacy for your company that continues well past your retirement, push your passion aside for a moment and open your mind to new ways of marketing to a new era of clients.

THE MORE YOU KNOW: COMPETITIVE INTELLIGENCE

KNOWLEDGE IS POWER. Staying aware of what your competition is doing in the marketplace makes good business sense. And in today's digital age, more information than you can dream of is just a few clicks away.

Imagine a tool that will send you an email nearly every time information about a competitor is posted on the Internet, often within minutes of the new post.

It exists, and it's called Google Alert. Visit google.com/alerts and enter search terms for your competitor (e.g., Smith Architects). Choose to just get news items, blog posts or everything that is posted. You can receive updates as soon as they happen, or you can opt for daily or weekly emails. If your competitor has a common name, and you are getting quite a few irrelevant alerts about unrelated businesses, try adding additional keywords to your search like your city. There are also paid services available, like Mention and Critical Mention, that do more in-depth monitoring of media, whether it is traditional or social media.

Facebook and Twitter allow you to stay current on your competitions' activity. Just "like" the Facebook pages and "follow" the Twitter profiles of your competitors to have their posts appear in your news feed.

For a true picture of how your competitors operate, you need to experience it yourself. There's no greater learning opportunity than to have your employees experience your competitors firsthand. Shop your competition. Ask them to report back to the team with details of their experiences so others can benefit from the research.

Interview new customers of yours regarding their experiences with your competitors to better understand what your competitors do well and where product/service opportunities exist. Most customers are happy to provide feedback that will help ensure you exceed their expectations. It's less critical that they attribute this information directly back to a specific competitor, and more important that they share their prior experiences with your competitors in general — the good, the bad and the ugly.

Track the open positions your competitors are posting as an indication of the firm's future growth or potential resource gaps. If you're competing with a publicly traded company, buy a share of stock, which will give you access to the company's financials.

Watch where your competitors are advertising and what messages they're using. If you're seeing repetition in a certain channel and message, then it is likely working.

Staying current on your competitors' activities isn't about keeping up with the Joneses. There is more to marketing than just doing more than the other guy. It's about being informed. The information you gather through your search should simply serve as one of several forms of input into your strategic sales and marketing planning efforts.

THE BRAIN BONE'S ATTACHED TO THE WALLET BONE

LOOKING AT YOUR BRAIN, neuromarketers can predict how you'll respond to advertising. While it may sound like mind reading, this relatively new, somewhat controversial field of research uses MRI scans and other technology to measure brain activity when consumers are exposed to products, brands and advertising. This tool can help marketers fine-tune marketing campaigns, strengthen brands and design better products.

Before you can benefit from this research, it is important to first understand that the "old brain" houses your most basic survival impulses and resists change. Your "middle brain" connects emotionally with the world. It's your "new brain," or the neocortex, where you process information logically, but your neocortex also has the weakest influence over your decisions.

Because of this, neuromarketers have uncovered that most consumers make buying decisions on survival or emotion before the new brain scrambles to logically justify these decisions. For example, one recent neuromarketing study determined that your old and middle brains make a purchasing decision a full seven seconds before you logically justify that decision.

Most business owners don't have a budget for neuromarketing, but what can we learn from the big brands that can make that investment?

The old brain makes decisions by weighting pain against what you stand to gain. Breaking the purchase into bite-size investments can reduce financial pain in the old brain, and if your product or service can add joy to your customers' lives, the old brain will see a lot to be gained in exchange for a little pain.

Your old brain is visual and responds quickly to images. Be thoughtful about your product's design and packaging, as well as images used in marketing. Remember to leverage as many of the five senses as possible. Consider a paper stock with an unusual feel for your business card or mailer, or a signature scent for your retail store. Incorporate more audio and video into your marketing. Tell your story visually first, and then add supporting copy with vivid sensory descriptions.

The middle brain remembers beginnings and endings. So, on a sales call make sure your opening and closing impressions create happy feelings that connect emotionally with your prospect.

The subconscious part of the brain wants to have what others have. Remember how ugly you thought Uggs were until everyone had a pair? Instead of telling your customers why you're great, have current customers tell your story, explaining the rewards and joy of using your product or working with your team. The old and middle brains will respond.

Neuromarketing researchers have determined that consumers cling to activities that make them feel in control — the rituals. Think about having your name called at Starbucks and dropping your cup into that oh-so-familiar coffee collar. It's comforting and familiar, isn't it?

What kind of ritual can you create for your business? Is it a signature treat for guests or a handwritten thank-you card after every customer interaction?

If your sales are flat, avoid the blame game and try playing the brain game.

THE PSYCHOLOGY OF PRICING

BUYERS HATE TO ADMIT IT, but we're emotional creatures, at least when it comes to decision making. We make a decision to buy based on emotional factors first, and afterward seek rational justification for the decision we've essentially already made. This same principle applies to how we assess your brand's price points as well — whether you sell products or services.

Be clear about your target audiences and their motivations for buying from you first, before you develop a pricing strategy. Are your customers buying value or prestige when selecting your brand? If you're a value brand, consider selecting a product price point just below one of the most common mental price barriers, which are $10, $20, $50, $100 and then $50 increments thereafter. If you're a luxury brand that makes consumers feel good about splurging, consider pricing right at or above these barrier levels.

Consumers tend to group prices according to the number of digits to the left of the decimal point. For example, most consumers see little if any difference between $16.50 and $19.50, and since both have two digits to the left of the decimal and fall beneath the $20 mental price barrier, why not charge the latter? Of course, they will see a difference between $16.50 and $66.50, so use good judgment.

The numbers to the right of the decimal also make an impression. Price points ending in seven or nine are seen as discount or limited-time offers. If all of your prices end in seven or nine, you're seen as a discount brand. If you're not a bargain brand, use this strategy sparingly. Products or services with prices ending in zero are perceived as higher quality or newer merchandise.

If you offer luxury products or services and are concerned about diluting the integrity of your brand with a discount pricing strategy but are looking for a special offer to drive sales, consider giving something away for free instead. For example, you could offer free shipping. It still makes customers feel as though they've gotten a special deal and can drive sales without devaluing your brand.

If you want customers to focus on the quality of what they are buying versus the money spent, remove the dollar signs from your prices and the cents. For example, instead of saying your product is $24.00, list the price as simply "24." You may notice upscale restaurants or boutiques putting this technique into practice.

High-end brands looking to discount might consider showing buyers both the original and sale prices. Just make sure the difference is easy for consumers to calculate, and ideally position the original price over a mental price barrier and the discount price under it. If the original price was $110, try offering the item for $80. Buyers can quickly calculate the $30 difference and will perceive that difference to be great.

Leverage these simple psychology-based pricing strategies to drive sales while protecting your brand.

THE PRICE IS RIGHT

HOW DO YOU KNOW when your product has the right price tag? Your pricing strategy is crucial to generating strong profitability. Before you can set the right price, you must first know the cost of producing and delivering your product or service, as well as the amount of operating expense required for every unit or service sold. These two figures combined make up your total cost. If you don't know your total cost, your pricing strategy is a mere dart game.

Once you have your total cost calculated, select a retail-pricing strategy that aligns most appropriately with your business category and competitive realities. For example, profit-margin pricing is determined by adding a desired profit margin to your total cost per unit or service sold. If your costs vary due to fluctuations in the cost of raw materials or labor, then your retail price would fluctuate accordingly.

Competitive pricing begins with "shopping" your competitors to determine their pricing points. If your consumers regard you as offering a unique experience, difficult-to-find products, or unrivaled service, then you may be in a position to price above your competitors. If you aren't sure how your customers perceive your offering in relation to competitors, ask them. Perception is reality.

Psychological pricing is based on your consumers' reaction to pricing, with the ultimate selection of a price they deem fair.

Once you've determined the price neighborhood you need to be in, consider what your price point will look like to the right of the decimal point, especially if you're in retail. Research shows consumers process price from left to right, placing the least emphasis on what follows the decimal. Numerous studies have shown that adding as much as $.99 to the end of your price point will not significantly reduce purchasing. However, consumers tend to see prices ending in $0.95, $0.97 or $0.99 as associated with sale prices — partially due to the odd-number ending. A price point ending in $0.50 would generally be perceived as a regularly priced item. Using an even price point, like $68.00, will reinforce a brand image of quality and sophistication.

Other pricing techniques include bundled pricing and loss-leader pricing. Bundled pricing involves grouping your products or services together for a single price. Often, bundling is used as a way to increase purchase volume at a slightly reduced margin. Loss-leader pricing generates traffic through the promotion of products or services, priced with little to no margin, in the hope consumers will purchase other higher-margin products or services as well.

Regardless of the pricing strategy selected, be sure to monitor your margins carefully each month, adjusting pricing accordingly. Keep in mind the impact regular discounting can have on your brand. You certainly don't want a scenario where your customers are waiting on your next discount before making a purchase.

ONE TEAM, ONE DREAM

TEAMWORK: every highly successful team gets just how important it is to propelling an organization forward. When true teamwork exists, all players are in lockstep.

Just like in sports, every player must be consistently in sync in each play for a maximum result. And the proverbial chain is only as strong as its weakest link.

However, most companies' sales and marketing efforts all too often operate in isolation within a company. Sales teams often don't see tangible value in marketing's work product and find marketing messaging inconsistent with their "real world" experiences with customers. Many a marketing team harbors frustration that the sales team doesn't leverage the tools it provides or value its contributions to the company. And typically neither defines its company's growth strategy in the same way.

It is a common challenge that's imperative to course correct if your company is to realize its full potential. Oracle reports that a recent Aberdeen Research study found that companies, which are best in class at aligning sales and marketing, experience a 20 percent annual revenue growth compared to a four percent decline by those out of alignment.

Alignment begins with a common understanding of your marketplace and your firm's position in it, which can be accomplished via research. Research your customers, prospects and influencers to understand how they see your company compared to competitors, where your brand is strong and weak in comparison, and what it will take for you to ultimately win and retain their business — from product adjustments to messaging changes to marketing delivery channels likely to break through.

Armed with these common truths about your company, next establish common definitions for every step in the sales cycle and clarify each team's role in contributing to those steps. After all, the ultimate role of sales and marketing is to contribute to the sales funnel and help advance prospects through the sales cycle.

As an example, how do you define a lead, a qualified lead and an opportunity? Is marketing's role simply lead generation? What role does marketing play in ensuring leads generated are qualified? Is the sales team also responsible for generating leads? If so, what lead generation activities are most effective and therefore the focus? What messaging, informed by the research, does everyone agree resonates most with prospects?

Equipped with consumer research, shared definitions and clear roles, next determine how you'll measure success for each member of your sales and marketing team. Also create collective marketing and sales team targets reported via a monthly dashboard to all, along with best practices in sales and marketing collaboration that ideally spur others. And finally, establish joint sales and marketing team growth projects allowing participating employees to see the business from the other's perspective.

ENSURE YOUR SALES AND MARKETING PLAN DELIVERS

TIRED OF CHASING your proverbial tail while you look for a sales and marketing plan that actually delivers? First, acknowledge that a silver bullet rarely exists. The solution, while not particularly sexy, can and will deliver growth, provided you trust the process and avoid the temptation to skip steps along the way.

Begin by researching what businesses in your category typically spend to maintain or grow market share. Most businesses plan on spending three percent of targeted sales one year from today on marketing and sales efforts, just to retain their current market share — by replacing lost customers with new ones, for example. However, most businesses that aspire to grow spend at least five percent of their targeted revenue for the next year on marketing and sales efforts.

Next, validate — through customer and prospect interviews and surveys — a few vital pieces of information upon which your plan will hinge, such as your differentiators, the companies your customers believe you compete against and how they differentiate, what messages resonate with customers, and what delivery channels they are most likely to notice. Avoid omitting this crucial step and you risk relying on your potentially biased assumptions. Gut-checks and guessing can condemn your plan to failure from the beginning.

Next define your goals and objectives for the year. Decide how you will measure your success by asking yourself what metrics you'll regularly review to gauge your success. Then determine the specific target audiences in which to focus in order to achieve the goals established, drafting customized messaging which will resonate with each. Your research should allow you to prioritize key messages in the order of importance to each target.

Determine the best strategies for reaching each of your targets and the tactics you will use to execute accordingly. For example, you might have a special offer for certain qualifying customers, or your sales team might need additional training.

Outline a realistic timeframe in which you are likely to see a return on each strategy planned. Strategies centered on training your sales team to improve existing customer cross-sell ratios often pay off more quickly than marketing strategies targeting new customer acquisition. Determining these "minimum payoff timeframes" and communicating them to your management team will help curb the impulse to derail from the plan before it has had ample time to deliver.

Prepare a report each quarter calculating key metrics and progress toward goal. Then refine your sales and marketing plan based on those findings. You may shift dollars away from one channel toward another generating better results.

If all of this sounds too daunting, causing you to reconsider a more common reactionary or shotgun approach, consider bringing in external support to guide you through the process so that you can make sure you get the most bang for your buck.

2

The brands deploying the most successful marketing strategies share these commonalities. They have claimed a unique brand territory. They have a distinct brand voice that resonates with buyers. They have a deep understanding of their target market – who they are, what makes them tick and why they buy. They have identified the most cost efficient and productive avenues for reaching them, and they focus on these channels in order to maintain an affordable cost of customer acquisition.

EXECUTE YOUR MARKETING STRATEGY

MARKING YOUR TERRITORY

I BET you didn't think your dog could teach you anything about marketing.

I've learned some important marketing lessons from mine, like the importance of marking your territory — though not in the literal sense. One of the most important fundamentals of marketing is to identify and claim ownership of a unique brand territory.

Claiming a brand territory means that you're putting a stake in the ground and letting your clients know what makes your company unique.

Defining that territory can be easier than it sounds. One great way to start is by surveying your customers, prospects and even your employees. Ask them all how they think your brand is different from your competitors. You'll also want to research the competitive "brandscape" by looking at the brand positioning of each of your competitors, as communicated on their website for example.

You're looking for a point of differentiation or brand territory that can stand up to these four criteria. You can uniquely claim it, meaning no competitors are making the same claim. It is an important point of distinction for your customers. You can easily prove it's a differentiator in just a few words. You can deliver on this differentiator consistently because it aligns with your company's internal realities.

Case in point: Tom Smith runs a business called Handyman Concierge, offering repair and renovation services. Tom's point of differentiation is that his crew shows up at a specific time, instead of during a broad timeframe, like "sometime between 12 and 5." If his crew doesn't arrive on time, the customer receives 10 percent off the price for every 15-minute delay — but Tom's prices are, on average, 10 percent higher than his competitors.

Tom's tagline is "On time or on our dime."

This fictitious example illustrates a legitimate differentiator. Tom has built a strategy around a concept that resonates with many of us: that time is valuable. He is able to charge a premium price for his services because most of us recognize that if we have to spend time away from work to wait for a repairman, we're losing real money.

Most importantly, his promise to be on time isn't hollow. Tom's scheduling guidelines and operations support this claim. He also built the crew's pay and incentive structure around this promise by offering bonuses if they are on time 95 percent of the time while maintaining high customer-satisfaction scores.

Because he follows through with this claim, Tom can charge a premium price that people are willing to pay. His differentiator is unique, it's important to customers, it's easy to prove and Tom's team can deliver on it consistently.

You can't claim your brand territory just with a catchy tagline. You must identify a differentiator that truly matters to your target audience, and then deliver that difference. Once you've found your unique selling point, develop your tagline and the marketing strategy to support it, so that you can mark your brand territory before someone else does.

RedRover co-founder, Julie Lunn, contributed to this column.

SPEAK UP

YOU HAVE A UNIQUE personality when you communicate — a style and tone that is entirely your own — and your company has a personality, too. Is your company's personality coming through in your communications?

If not, you are missing an opportunity to connect with clients in an authentic way.

Why don't business communications reflect company personality? It's actually difficult to remove personality from communications, but companies often fear that customers and prospects won't understand or appreciate their personality. We've also been trained to believe that business is serious. Because of this, most companies depersonalize communications to the point that no one wants to read them.

Finding your company's voice isn't difficult, but you do need to give thought to these questions. What is your company's culture? What are the personality traits within your business? How do you want customers and prospects to see you? How would you describe your company? Do you want others to see you as humorous and bold, caring and approachable, or even edgy and trendy?

Moosejaw, an outdoor gear retailer with a strong online presence, has mastered the art of branding with a company voice. One of its strategies has been to pack a preprinted note with every order featuring a clever message, like this one: "If you are actually reading this note, you should be super happy. First, you have received your order, reading is fun, and getting something in the mail (even if you bought it yourself) has got to make the day better. Second, I put your order together all by myself."

The note is not only fun, but it makes you like Moosejaw more because of the message. It works because it is unexpected and memorable.

While it is clear everyone who gets a package gets the same or a similar note, it's refreshing not to get the typical promotional flyer. It makes you feel like there are real humans on the other side of your shipment. The tone is casual, with a slightly edgy sense of humor, which reflects the personality of the Moosejaw brand — a personality that appeals to the company's target audience.

Let's face it; we all enjoy being a customer of a company that dares to have an interesting personality. More importantly, it makes the company stand out in the market, giving it a serious competitive advantage.

At RedRover, Rover is our voice. He explains our sales and marketing philosophies by obvious overuse of doggone corny expressions, along with the occasional dog command like "speak" or "fetch." Rover is a hybrid of the personalities of our firm's employees, and he reflects our sense of humor. We bring this voice to life in our written communications, website, notecards and even in our office decor.

If you're looking to stand apart from your competition, there may be no better way than creating a unique voice. It doesn't have to be silly, fun or cool. Even serious tones can carry a unique quality, engaging your customers and prospects to make them feel closer to you.

RICHARD BRANSON ON PERSONAL BRANDING

MANY OF THE TOP-PERFORMING CEOs in the world, as determined by Harvard Business Review, are names that aren't exactly common fodder for dinner conversation. They know how to create long-term value for their companies, but many of them don't focus on creating their own personal brands.

Personal branding may not be essential for leadership within large corporations, but for small businesses, having a well-branded CEO/owner at the helm can make a difference. It can help differentiate your brand, creating a stronger connection with the marketplace. It can result in prospects specifically seeking you out, instead of just hunting for the lowest-priced option.

As a CEO/owner, your decisions about your personal brand should hinge on your long-term intentions for your company. If your goal is ultimately to sell the company, then crafting a strong personal brand can make it challenging to sell without sounding alarms among customers about your absence. Think about Steve Jobs. Investors understand this, too. If you plan to step back from your leadership role soon, a strong personal brand can actually devalue your company.

However, if you are planning to stay with your company for the long haul, then a personal brand that emphasizes your expertise makes sense. Your personal brand could allow the marketplace to relate more easily to you and your company. Customers might like to know what makes you tick, and they might even empathize with you more. However, once you've connected your personal brand to your business, personal or professional missteps can lead to public scrutiny.

If you want to build a personal brand to support your business, begin by determining your mantra. Think of this as a short statement that you'll use to communicate your brand. Richard Branson's mantra can be found within his Twitter profile: "Tie-loathing adventurer and thrill seeker, who believes in turning ideas into reality. Otherwise known as Dr. Yes at @virgin!"

Creating your mantra can be challenging, but try using this formula: Description + Function + Emotion. Your description identifies your industry. Your function explains the service you offer, and what makes you stand out from the crowd. Your emotional appeal emphasizes how people benefit from working with you, how you make them feel, or how they describe you.

Consider asking colleagues, employees and friends to describe you in 10 words or fewer to help find the key words you should use in your mantra.

Next, tell the story behind that mantra in words and pictures consistently — through each social media post you make, the content you develop and promote, and each personal interaction. Grow your network by connecting with people who will find value in your content, and continuously evolve your content to increase its relevancy to the people in your network.

Promoting your personal brand in the market can offer your company a strong competitive advantage, but make certain to manage your reputation carefully. Understand how the lines between your personal and professional brands can blur together.

A CALLING CARD
THAT SPEAKS VOLUMES

FOR THOSE IN MARKETING, there is never enough time in the day to get it all done, so savvy marketers seek passive marketing strategies to complement their more active strategies. Passive marketing is like having a secret ally working for you 24/7.

Passive marketing strategies, much like passive income streams, require virtually no upkeep.

Once you've made the initial investment, they continue to work behind the scenes. One of the simplest passive marketing strategies is to fully leverage your business card. Why not create one that speaks for you long after it has left your hand? The trick is to create a unique card with perceived value — a business card that is so creative, recipients want to hang on to it, refer to it later, or share it with colleagues.

So how do you "go big" on one of these small cards?

Start with the basics. Clean up your contact information. Remember that less is more. Your website, email and phone number are generally enough. Since your address is only a click away, resist the urge to clutter your card with it.

Next, you should consider both the form and function of your business card. If you run a lawn service, print your contact information on a small business card-sized envelope with grass seeds inside. If you're marketing a bakery, create edible cards. Do you sell all-natural furniture? Make your business card from natural wood. Marketing a bookstore? Let your card serve as a bookmark. If you own an optometry practice, consider a card that doubles as a magnifying glass. Does your painting company pride itself on masking abilities? Reinforce that differentiator by having card recipients pull back a piece of masking tape to reveal your contact information.

Never leave the back of your card blank. The back of your business card is prime real estate that you need to put to good use, even if it's just with a creative, professional photo of your product or an interesting fact chosen to challenge or inform readers.

Research shows that when you can engage multiple senses, there is a better chance that people will remember you. Make your card more tactile with an unusual paper stock, die cut or with embossing, which can give a three-dimensional effect. Your local printer can create a custom die cut to allow you to convert your brand name into a stencil. You might also consider an unusual card shape such as round, square or even the shape of your logo. For example, if you own a coffee shop, consider designing your card in the shape of a cup of joe.

Turn your business card into a passive marketing strategy that speaks for you long after it's handed off by throwing tradition out the window and getting creative.

MARKETING FROM THE HEART

NO OTHER TECH GIANT understood the importance of investing emotionally in a brand, instead of in a product, better than Steve Jobs — and that understanding is at the heart of Apple's rise to market dominance. Jobs believed that the essence of a brand isn't rational or logical; it's all about how the brand makes people feel emotionally.

Take Nike, for example.

Jobs said, "Nike sells a commodity; they sell shoes. And yet when you think of Nike you feel something different than a shoe company. In their ads, as you know, they don't ever talk about the product… What's Nike do in their advertising? They honor great athletes, and they honor great athletics. That's who they are. That is what they are about."

Finding your brand's emotional essence means that you have to understand objectively what makes your brand unique. True differentiation is defined as something you offer the marketplace that competitors can't claim, that you can easily prove, and that really matters to prospective customers. Conducting market research ensures that your customers agree with the differentiator you've identified, and that they value that difference.

Once you've identified what makes your brand different, examine how that differentiator makes your customers feel about your brand emotionally. When Jobs spoke about Apple, for example, he focused on the emotions and beliefs at the core of the company, saying, "What we're about isn't making boxes for people to get their jobs done — although we do that well. We can do that almost better than anyone else can in some cases. But Apple's about something more than that. Apple, at the core, its core value is we believe that people with passion can change the world for the better."

The Apple branding focuses on this core value. Apple's advertising seems to say, "Seeking creative, free-spirited people with passion who believe they are capable of anything and can change the world for the better." That's the emotional essence of Apple's brand. It's about so much more than a logo.

Some differentiators don't have a strong emotional voice. Many companies claim that their great customer service makes them different, for example. You can't easily prove, however, that your company is unique in this regard until prospects experience your customer service personally, which can only happen after they've become customers. This is one reason customer service isn't a strong differentiator. More importantly, customer service rarely inspires passionate, positive emotions in consumers.

If you want to find a stronger emotional differentiator, ask yourself how your brand is affecting your consumers emotionally today. What emotions do you want to inspire in your customers?

Even early on, Jobs understood the importance of emotional marketing. He said, "Marketing is about values. It's a complicated and noisy world, and we're not going to get a chance to get people to remember much about us. No company is. So we have to be really clear about what we want them to know about us."

Your company may only have one chance to make an impression, making it essential to deliver a clear, meaningful message capable of standing the test of time.

AIM HIGH

MANY SMALL BUSINESS OWNERS aren't sure what their prospective clients have in common, so they don't know how to identify their target markets. Target marketing is about segmenting your prospective customers, and then choosing a delivery method and message with each segment in mind. It is generally more efficient to attack a single segment or two at a time, especially when you have a limited marketing budget.

Begin by identifying the top 10 percent of your most profitable customers. Next, think about what they have in common. Consider their demographic profile, including their age, gender, geography, education and average house-hold income. Finally, sharpen this profile by looking at psychographic traits, like values, interests, activities, attitudes and lifestyles. For example, is your target conservative or liberal? What hobbies do they pursue? What causes do they support? Are they fun loving, environmentally minded, family oriented or cutting-edge?

If you don't know your most profitable customers quite this well, don't despair. There are a few easy ways to gather this information. For example, a data or list broker can take contact information on your most profitable customers and add demographic and psychographic data to it. Once you have this information, look for the commonalities. You can also survey your most profitable customers yourself to determine their habits and preferences.

With this target market profile in hand, you will have a much better idea of how to reach these kinds of customers, and what messages will appeal most to them. Be sure to give thought to an appropriate reach and frequency for each segment you're targeting. Reach is the number of prospects within that segment who see or hear your message. Frequency is the number of times those targeted prospects hear or see your message. Focus on achieving optimum reach and frequency for one target segment before expanding to additional segments. And by all means, you don't always have to focus on traditional ways of reaching these prospects.

Let's take the example of the CEO of a boutique personal training studio that focuses on runners as a specific niche. Instead of investing heavily in advertising or direct mail, as bigger brands in this space often do, this owner came up with a creative, highly targeted solution.

While much running gear is indeed purchased online these days, specialized running shoes are still often bought in a retail location, allowing a fit expert to help the runner choose a style of shoe that works in light of his particular stride and running challenges. So this personal training CEO and her staff visited every running shoe store in the city and tried on numerous shoe styles with each visit. After placing shoes back into their boxes, they also placed business cards inside which touted their focus on runners.

Runners trying on the shoes saw the cards and may have assumed other runners used the training studio. Regardless, the messages were getting into prospective buyers' hands when they had running on their minds. This tactic gave the studio credibility and generated more calls than they could handle.

In the words of Henry David Thoreau, "In the long run, men hit only what they aim at. Therefore, they had better aim at something high." Why not raise your aim by reaching your most profitable customers with target marketing?

THE NEXT-GENERATION CUSTOMER

FINDING YOUR IDEAL CLIENTS may feel a little like searching for the holy grail. Every business is seeking out these ideal prospects, but the traditional methods for identifying them may not always be the most effective.

Conventional approaches involve examining the profile of the top 10 percent of your most profitable customers. Next, you would identify the demographic qualities they share as a group so that you can look for other prospects that share those demographics. This method is called customer profiling.

While this can pay off in the short run, it's not enough. You may be missing a bigger opportunity. Who are the ideal customers that will support your business in the future? In order to be successful, you also need to attract the next generation of clients. It is easy to focus on the customers who love you the most now, but you must also pay attention to the generation that is coming next so that you can maintain your position in the marketplace.

However, the same tried-and-true marketing strategies you've used in the past to attract Baby Boomers may fall flat with Gen X — and Millennials are a whole different story.

There are fundamental experiences we share as a collective generation:

experiences that shape our values, how we prefer to communicate, what we buy, and what factors influence our purchasing decisions the most. These shared experiences color each generation's world, shaping their behavior. Wars, the economy, scientific or technological advancements, social tragedies, memorable moments in entertainment, changing political structures, or sociological shifts influence and transform each generation in profound ways.

Marketing with these differences in mind will allow you to frame your product or service's benefits in a way that aligns with a unique generation's values and preferences. Generational marketing not only increases your ability to connect with each generation in a meaningful way, it also leads to increased customer loyalty and a stronger return on your marketing investment.

Levis-Strauss learned about the importance of generational marketing the hard way in the late 1990s. Baby Boomers had always loved their jeans, and the company had gotten accustomed to being on top. They weren't paying attention to the needs of Gen X and the Millennials. Before they knew it, Levis had become "your parent's jeans." As you might imagine, this didn't appeal to the younger generations, and their market share dropped accordingly.

How can you make sure your brand is relevant to your best customers of tomorrow? Can you reach these prospective customers before it's too late? Never take your eye off your future customers, speaking to them in their own language and reaching them where they live.

THE SIGNIFICANCE OF GENERATIONAL MARKETING

COLLECTIVE EXPERIENCES shape each generation — whether it's World War II or Vietnam, the election of JFK or the scandal of Watergate, the invention of the television or the rise of the Internet, and even listening to the Beatles or Bruce Springsteen growing up. The experiences of our formative years influence each generation's values and core beliefs, their preferred methods of communication, the products they need, and ultimately, their buying decisions. Understanding these shared beliefs is at the heart of generational marketing.

Big brands appreciate the need to understand generational nuances. That's why we are surprised when they make devastating generational marketing blunders, like marketing to current customers with little more than a nod to the upcoming generation of consumers. The customer buying from you today is important, but the next big thing for your industry is the next generation. Ignore the rising generation, and you'll risk brand irrelevancy.

If big brands with their resources can make this misstep, smaller companies should take heed to avoid following suit.

Prior to the late 1960s, Playtex owned the girdle market. However, Baby Boomer women, who were just beginning to control a decent percentage of undergarment purchases, didn't value confining undergarments. They also had great influence over purchases made by their parents, ultimately influencing their mothers to opt for more comfortable alternatives to the girdle. Playtex wasn't in touch with the needs of its next generation of customers. The brand didn't research Baby Boomer's needs or target its marketing to that next generation accordingly — and it paid for the mistake dearly.

Eastman Kodak is a more recent casualty of the generational marketing war. Despite inventing the first digital camera, Kodak was fearful to stray too far from its roots in film and film-based cameras. It was slow to fully embrace digital technology and commercialize it. Basically, Eastman Kodak wasn't listening to its next generation of customers. If asked, Gen X would have shouted "no more film."

By the time Eastman Kodak turned its sights toward the digital world, the brand had become irrelevant to Generation X and Millennials. The financial investment to convince the next generations otherwise, combined with competitive pressure, was insurmountable.

Kodak declared bankruptcy in 2012.

These are serious lessons to learn. Don't lose sight of your future customers. Listen to feedback on your product and service developments often, and never forget to target your marketing so it resonates with the next generation.

BOOMERS – REBELS WITH A CAUSE

THERE WERE MORE than 77 million babies born between 1946 and 1964 in the United States. Even though a White House study confirms that Millennials finally outpaced Boomers in 2014, Boomers are still a force to be reckoned with. Before you can market to them, though, you have to understand them.

Baby Boomers share common experiences such as economic prosperity, postwar optimism, suburban expansion, the sexual revolution, and rock and roll. Individuality, expressionism, adventure and breaking the rules are classic Boomer traits. Music was a way to express their unique generational identity, and they bought the Beatles, Hendrix and Motown albums in droves. Young Boomers saw life as full of possibilities; the economy was solid, and jobs were plentiful. There was a radio, and eventually, a TV in nearly every living room. Boomers felt entitled to enjoyment and fulfillment.

Over time, though, their optimism was shaken by the assassinations of JFK and Martin Luther King Jr., the Watergate scandal, the Apollo 13 disaster and the Vietnam War. Boomers began to question authority and conformity. Opposing discrimination, Boomers led the civil rights and women's movements. Many vehemently opposed the Vietnam War. Protesting was commonplace.

Even today, given a worthwhile cause, they'll fight for it like no other generation.

They enjoyed big jobs, salaries and houses, only to have them stripped away by corporate failures and downsizing. Now, many are struggling to stabilize their careers and finances before retiring.

What concerns Baby Boomers the most? Growing old is their number one concern. They also feel guilty for not having spent enough time with their kids. Sandwiched between caring for both their kids and parents, they are stressed out and feel spread very thin. Time is a luxury.

Making them feel passé or calling attention to their age unnecessarily will offend Baby Boomers. But how can you engage them?

You can provide products or services that free up their time, improve their appearance or give them more energy and better health. Half of all Boomers have grandkids they like spending money on, so offer them experiences to enjoy with their grandchildren.

Nothing beats face-to-face communication when selling to Boomers. This generation also relies heavily on referrals from trusted social and professional advisers. Direct mail, e-mail and the Internet are also very effective.

Harley Davidson has historically been a brand that gets Boomers. Life with a Harley isn't about Bingo night and fading into the backdrop of life. There's a brand cachet with owning a Harley. Its owners are portrayed as cool, rebellious, risk takers with a never-grow-old spirit.

This motorcycle brand knows just how to appeal to stressed out Baby Boomers. But this savvy brand isn't sitting on its laurels, only targeting this single demographic — as that is inevitably a recipe for a future brand in crisis. Targeted marketing is also actively deployed against Gen X and Millennials — the brand's next generation of customer — featuring music, nostalgia and sentiments uniquely appealing to these generations.

Now that's a strategy you can take to the bank.

X MARKS THE SPOT

BORN FROM 1965 TO 1976, Gen Xers are entering their peak earning years and, more importantly, haven't yet formed strong brand loyalties, so smart brands are prioritizing their Gen X marketing strategy.

As a member of Generation X, I can appreciate why our generation is characterized as having a survivor mentality. Skeptical and pragmatic, Xers have witnessed crumbling political, corporate and family structures. With rising divorce rates and financial uncertainty, more Xers were latchkey kids raised by working (and often single) parents. Having seen all of these dramatic life changes, it's no wonder they embrace risk and question authority.

Gen X saw millions of families dismantled after recessions and corporate downsizing hit their Baby Boomer parents hard. As a result, Gen X lost faith in the institution of marriage, but they also became disillusioned with corporations. By essentially raising themselves, Generation X developed a steely self-reliance. Many members of Gen X are entrepreneurs, choosing to make their own way rather than trusting corporate entities. In fact, Gen X has started more than two-thirds of U.S. businesses. At the same time, feeling orphaned as latchkey kids, Gen Xers want brands to prove they are willing to invest in a relationship.

Since MTV and radio were like surrogate parents for Gen X, savvy marketers often evoke nostalgia with this generation's music.

Gen X is also tech savvy. From the bag phone to the iPhone, from vinyl to digital music, from the Tandy 1000 to the MacBook, Gen X is able to adapt to rapid changes. In fact, they thrive on technological stimuli — through their laptops, cell phones, iPad and social-media networks. Without technology, they're bored.

Because Gen X is less comfortable with debt, they appreciate a good value — and when they find it, they will tell their friends in droves. Because of this, word of mouth is the strongest way to reach Gen X. Email and the Internet, including social media, are the next strongest communication channels, along with multimedia marketing. Direct mail is more effective for Gen X than with Millennials, but less effective than it is with Boomers.

Gen X speaks the language of straightforward sound bites. This generation is used to solving its own problems, so show Gen Xers how your product or service can help solve real problems. Information is power to Gen X.

Volkswagen channeled its inner "Xer" in one of the most memorable and many believe, the most shared, Super Bowl commercial in recent time — called "The Force." The spot opens showing a child donning a Darth Vader costume and accompanied by Star Wars music who tries in vain to use "the Force" to power everything from the exercise bike to the dog to the dryer. Almost at the brink of frustration, "Vader" uses his powers on the family Volkswagen with success and a well-timed assist from Dad using the car's remote start feature.

This ad worked because of the nostalgia and emotional connection generated by the music and the Star Wars theme and because Generation X loves a practical, value-oriented product. It was also a beautifully understated commercial, demonstrating the brand doesn't take itself too seriously, which aligns with Gen X's disdain for overstatement and hype.

If Gen X is a strong demographic for your business, why market to them as if they're Baby Boomers or Millennials? Remember that X marks the spot.

THE REAL POWER OF GEN Y

COLLECTIVELY, GENERATIONS SHARE cultural experiences that shape their values, technological developments that affect how they prefer to communicate, and lifestyle expectations that inform their purchasing decisions. There are a myriad of factors that influence which products and brands appeal to each generation — and which ones don't — and understanding these differences is central to generational marketing.

Of all the generations, Millennials are the most misunderstood, both in the workplace and in the marketplace. Often described as entitled, Millennials have an inaccurate reputation for demonstrating a less-than-stellar work ethic, born from helicopter parenting and participation trophies. However, there's much more to Millennials than meets the eye.

Born between the early 1980s and the year 2000, Millennials now, in 2015, make up one quarter of the U.S. population according to the U.S. Census Bureau. They are more than 80 million strong, making this generation the largest, according to a 2014 Millennials report issued by The Council of Economic Advisors. Millennials were shaped by the creation of the Internet and e-commerce, the Columbine shooting and 9/11, and not least of all, reality television.

As children, the average Millennial spent five hours a day engaging with media, including television, computers, video games and music. Using technology is like breathing to them, so an outdated or poorly functioning website can be incredibly frustrating for this generation. Millennials are relying less on TV as they age, preferring to use streaming services like Netflix and Hulu instead. With digital music taking over radio listenership among this segment, it is increasingly difficult to reach this group through traditional TV and radio ads.

Instead, Millennials respond well when they feel they've stumbled across your message by themselves. For example, Red Bull has been known to enlist well-connected students to create buzz on college campuses by talking about the brand and throwing Red Bull parties. Sneaker manufacturer Vans has marketed to Gen Y by building skate parks for their communities.

These community-building marketing strategies are important. Even though Millennials are quick to make purchases, they don't like traditional sales pitches. They appreciate a more authentic approach that speaks to their core values. Especially because of the tragedies that occurred during their most formative years, like 9/11, Millennials want to cure the world of its problems. Focusing on your brand's vision and greater purpose can help you connect with Millennials in a meaningful way that inspires a deep sense of loyalty. Cultivating this loyalty is crucial because Millennials are more loyal to their favorite brands than any other generation before them.

For most companies, Gen Y is a vast untapped market. If you want to tick them off, talk down to them, deliver a traditional sales pitch, or give them disappointing technology. If you want Millennials to become your brand advocates, use humor to show your brand doesn't take itself too seriously, make them feel respected and make them feel like they're a part of a positive change that's important to the larger world. Right now, as young adults, Millennials are poised to have profound impact on society — and on your bottom line.

MARS AND VENUS

RESEARCH FROM NIELSEN NEUROFOCUS, reported by TechVibes, has uncovered significant differences in the way men and women make purchasing decisions. In fact, the way men and women process information is fundamentally different.

Female brains are wired for big-picture thinking and multi-tasking. This means that women are likely to be engaged in at least one other activity while viewing your ad, so your key message needs to be clear. You would also be wise to repeat your message where possible. Women's brains are hard-wired for gut reasoning and empathy, so you need to connect with them on emotional levels.

It can be easy to apply this research to your own business. If you represent a nonprofit, for example, knowing that women influence the majority of charitable giving, you should lean toward emphasizing emotional reasons to donate, instead of using facts and figures to tell your story.

Male brains lean farther away from intuition. Men are goal-oriented shoppers, and they're willing to pay a higher price to get purchases checked off their lists. Provide logical solutions to their problems, and you're likely to capture their attention. A company that has provided a simple, logical solution to a man's razor needs is Dollar Shave Club. Sign up online, and receive new razors monthly. With no commitments or add-on fees, as well as catchy advertising during the Super Bowl, this company quickly made a name for itself.

Men are also more competitive by nature, so you can hit home more often by explaining how your product or service can provide an advantage over personal or professional "competitors."

Because men want to limit shopping time, they may pop into a store for just an item or two. Men rarely browse or compare prices. They are, however, more likely than women to make impulse purchase decisions at the cash register, assuming the purchases are something they can use, which may help them avoid another shopping trip. It's more practical to build your point-of-sale displays with men in mind.

Obvious calls to action, like emphasizing that the offer expires soon, may motivate men more often, but this pressure can be a turn-off for women. Women seek social harmony, and so this kind of hard sell is less effective with them.

Just as with any form of target marketing, there are always exceptions to the rule. Not all men or women are preconditioned for the exact same type of gender-influenced decision-making. However, applying these marketing principles to your advertising campaigns will ensure your messaging better resonates with your target market.

GOOGLE: GO MOBILE OR GO HOME

IN EARLY 2015, Google dramatically shook up the way it delivered search results by shifting emphasis toward mobile-friendly websites. If your site wasn't mobile optimized, you might have experience a radical decline in your ranking, and your business probably suffered — but this change was inevitable considering that the number of mobile Internet users outpaced desktop users in 2014 for the first time in history, according to CNN Money.

What makes a mobile-friendly website? According to Google, your site must avoid software uncommon to mobile devices, like Adobe Flash. Your text must be readable without zooming, and content must automatically adjust to fit smaller screens without requiring users to scroll horizontally or zoom. Finally, Google-approved mobile-friendly sites ensure that links are large enough and far enough apart that the user can easily tap them on-screen.

There are two ways to approach the creation of a mobile-friendly website. Ideally, you would build a mobile-responsive website. You could also develop a separate mobile friendly version of your website. While those two solutions may sound similar, they are quite different.

Building a mobile-responsive website means no matter which page of your site a user accesses on a mobile device, each one will automatically resize itself for optimum viewing on the particular device in use, whether it is a smart phone, a full-size tablet, a mini-tablet or a laptop. Let's say, for example, your responsive website generally displays three columns of content on each page when viewed on your desktop, but when viewed on your tablet, that content automatically shifts to a two-column format to avoid any need to scroll horizontally.

While this responsive option is certainly ideal, it can be a challenging upgrade for an existing site depending upon how it was originally developed. Another option is to create a mobile-only version of your website. Special mobile sites have reduced content, large buttons and a focus on just the content mobile users want most, like contact information and driving directions. Your site can be coded to automatically detect a mobile viewer and deliver this separate mobile version to users. However, this means you have two different sites to maintain, which could actually end up costing more in the long run, if you factor in your time.

Deciding which solution makes the most sense for your business begins with an assessment of the volume of mobile users on your site and how they typically interact with it. This data is typically available through most website reporting tools. No matter which path you choose, you need to capitalize on this considerable Google change before your competition.

CONVERT WEB TRAFFIC TO SALES

EVERYONE NEEDS an online presence to survive in the digital age, but how do you know that your investment is actually performing?

Before you can answer this question, you need to shift your mindset. Don't focus on simply generating more traffic. You need to pay attention to the kind of traffic that converts to actual sales. Traffic that doesn't lead to a sale doesn't have much value.

Don't take the "kitchen sink" approach, where you clutter the home page to tell buyers every reason they should buy. Instead, focus on the one most important reason. Remember that consumer attention spans are at an all-time low, so visual storytelling has a higher likelihood of engaging with most demographics than traditional paragraph-form text.

You also need to make sure there is a realistic next step that visitors can take on your site by making your call to action perfectly clear. If you're selling a $100 product, it's conceivable that a prospect's next step is to buy. On the other hand, if you have a law practice with a more complex offering and a higher price point, the sales cycle is more involved. A realistic next step might be to request a consultation with one of your attorneys or download an informative article written by your staff to continue the conversation.

Our eyes are naturally drawn to the upper-left hand corner of a website first. Consider using that prominent real estate for your opt-in newsletter request to boost the number of email addresses you capture, which can later be used to convert visitors to customers through an email campaign.

When designing your site, select a couple of conversion elements for A–B testing. For example, place your "Order Now" button in one spot during the first week of your test, then place it in a different location during week two. Or better yet, serve up one version of your home page to half of your site visitors and a second version to the rest during the same timeframe. Compare which option was most successful in drawing attention. For a snapshot of how people are using your site, consider ClickTale.com, which maps your site visitors' mouse movements and pinpoints where visitors are on your site when they leave it. This tool arms you with information to make adjustments that improve conversion.

You should also allow customers to share reviews of your products and services on your site, which can significantly improve sales rates due to the third-party validation. Remember that the time it takes for a website to load is crucial. Most Internet users won't wait more than two seconds for a page to display. Other studies suggest that a one-second delay in page response can reduce your traffic by double-digit numbers. Reducing your traffic translates to fewer opportunities to make a sale.

Use these strategies to improve sales conversions, but remember that what works for your business may be unique. Monitor your successes and missteps through free reporting tools like Google Analytics, and adjust your approach accordingly.

ARE TRADITIONAL WEBSITES DEAD?

REPORTS OF THE DEATH of corporate websites have been greatly exaggerated, but there's no denying that traditional sites are experiencing declines in traffic.

WebTrends analyzed the number of unique visits to Fortune 100 websites. 68 percent of these sites experienced declines in unique visitors compared to the previous year, with an average decline of over 20 percent.

The study points to Facebook as a primary reason for this decline. Since Facebook's content is updated more regularly and there's a greater opportunity for consumer engagement there, the market is often electing to visit your Facebook page instead of your website. Today's websites need to operate more like Facebook, with multiple content updates each week and more opportunities to easily share, like or comment on that content.

If you have a traditional corporate site, odds are that most of your site visitors are quickly scanning your home page, and then leaving because they aren't looking for promotional information. They want practical, useful information, like best practices, informative facts and customer stories. Your site should function like a hub for interaction, and you should consider yourself more of a publisher versus marketer as a result.

Few brands are doing this well, with InboundWriter.com reporting in 2013 that 90 percent of most website traffic comes from just 10 to 20 percent of a website's content. Imagine the number of site visitors you could generate if 50 percent of your web content was socially engaging.

Many advertisers are actually using their Facebook pages as their primary ad campaign call to action, instead of their websites, with some small businesses using Facebook in lieu of a brand website all together. After all, social platforms are driving brand recommendations like never before.

Regardless, most brand marketers can't rely exclusively on social media channels of communication for all of their brand messaging, because on social media, they can't have as much messaging control. Websites continue to play a necessary role in establishing a strong, recognizable brand, but it's social media that is driving real business results for many companies.

An effective social media strategy should involve actively participating in relevant online communities where your target market is already spending its time. You should also work to build a community on those social media platforms for consumers interested in your products or services, where your brand can be established as an expert on the subject.

Being active and engaged allows new prospective customers to experience your brand firsthand before they ever purchase your product or service. Sometimes, that social experience is enough to create a sale on its own, but positive social media experiences can also drive consumers to your website, where they make their purchasing decisions.

The success of your brand's online presence depends in large part on your social media engagement.

GETTING TO PAGE ONE

WE ALL KNOW INTUITIVELY that a strong search engine ranking can impact traffic to your website, but just how important is it that your website is one of the first links in the search results?

According to ProtoFuse, 90 percent of people don't click past the first page of search results, and the top three results on page one, excluding paid ads, account for 60 percent of the clicks. What can you do to improve your search traffic? The answer is search engine optimization, which is often abbreviated as SEO.

One way to improve your placement in search engine results is to purchase ads through Google, guaranteeing you a featured position at the top or right of the organic search results, which is paid SEO. However, "organic" SEO is generally seen as the stronger option. Driving organic SEO means deploying strategies for improving your search ranking without paying for your placement.

Before you can optimize your website to get strong organic search results, you'll need to establish website traffic reporting. Using a free tool like Google Analytics will show you what's working with your website already. Google Analytics will provide you with the percentage of traffic generated from search engines and the most popular keyword combinations driving users to your site.

Next, utilize free tools such as Google Trends or Google Insights to compare the number of searches for one keyword combination against another in your region. Once you know what search terms are popular, you can use these keywords throughout the copy on your website. When it comes to SEO, original content has tremendous value. Search engines can tell whether your content is original, or whether it's been repurposed from another site. If your content is original, you will get higher placement in the search results.

If you're looking for a specific page of your website to rank highly for a particular search term, use that term in the title of that page. The page title is coded behind the scenes on your website, and can be different than the words that are actually displayed on the page. You should also include a site map on your website, which will allow search engines to find all the important pages on your website, and help them understand your site's hierarchy. Finally, all the images on your site should have short descriptions, called "alt tags," that tell the search engines what they portray.

Search engines also love blogs with up-to-date content, often rewarding those sites with higher rankings. Regularly post blog content that uses common search terms. Promote your blog posts through social media channels. Search engines love that, too.

When it comes to leaders in the search space, Google is a behemoth, capturing roughly 64 percent of U.S. searches in 2015, but don't put all of your eggs in Google's basket. Google regularly updates its secretive algorithm, and the next change could drive your website to page five of the search results. Just as you diversify your investment portfolio, ensure you're getting traffic from other sources such as your email newsletter, social media profiles, blog or local online directories.

GOOGLE GETS INSIDE OUR HEADS

IN THE WORLD OF SEARCH ENGINES, Google is clearly king. Marketing professionals across the globe give this tech giant most of their search marketing attention by far. Every time Google makes a change to its secretive algorithm, search engine marketers scramble to assess the impact of the update and adjust their strategies accordingly. After all, according to one recent study, if your website isn't on the first page of Google's search results, 90 percent of users will never see it.

While Google's algorithm changes often, the company's ultimate vision — to deliver users the fastest and most relevant responses to search queries — has never blinked. While many of Google's advancements in search technology have allowed the search engine to overcome manipulative "black hat" strategies that tried to game their search results, Google has recently begun to tweak its algorithm to function more like our brains, becoming more conversational in nature.

Most of the time, when we head to Google, we're looking for the answer to a question. If you want to know how to choose the best type of window coverings for your new home, for example, you would naturally ask, "How do I pick window coverings for my home?" However, in the past, you would need keywords like "window treatment selection guide" to get the results you wanted. Google doesn't just want to give you results that are relevant to what you actually said; Google wants to respond to what you intended to say, even when that doesn't match what you wrote.

In a way, Google is learning how to read our minds better than ever before. For example, right now, if you search for the word "advertisement," Google will give you the definition of the word in the search results before it provides any other information. However, if you search for the word "advertisements" instead, Google leads with images. Why? Google is assuming that if you're searching for the plural "advertisements," you want examples and images of ads. If you search for the singular "advertisement," it assumes you just want to know what the word means. Even though the only difference is one letter on the end of the word, the search results change to reflect what Google thinks you meant, not what you actually typed.

The idea of Google trying to replicate our thought patterns might make you a bit uncomfortable; however, when you think of the growing number of searches initiated by voice command through Siri or Google Glass, you begin to see that it's necessary. We don't naturally speak in neatly organized key words. The Google team is intent on returning results that align with the user's real intent for the search. If you want your page to continue to be ranked highly by Google's newest algorithms, writing conversational content is the key.

YOU'VE GOT EMAIL

WHILE EMAIL MARKETING may have lost a bit of luster given the instant gratification of social media, it's still alive and well. In fact, in 2013, McKinsey and Company reported that email is 40 times better than Facebook and Twitter at acquiring new customers. Why? While social media marketing has some advantages, email marketing can be more easily targeted and often requires less time to reach a similarly sized target audience. It's also easier to measure, test and optimize.

It should be no surprise, then, that according to eMarketer, email marketing was the most effective digital marketing channel for customer retention in the United States in 2014. According to *BtoB Magazine*, 59 percent of business-to-business marketers say email is the most effective channel for generating revenue, and 49 percent of marketers invest more time and resources on email than on other channels.

Every successful email campaign begins with a solid list of email addresses. Build your list with qualified contacts that have indicated a real interest in your product or services, but think beyond basic website home page enrollment when it comes to growing your list. Capture email addresses at offline events such as networking activities or speaking engagements; offer premium content on your website, like informative articles or research, in exchange for basic contact information; and encourage email subscription at the time of purchase or when an online contact form is submitted.

Consider sending subscribers who haven't clicked a link in your emails for several months a renewal email that will engage them again. If customers do opt-out of future emails, prompt them to explain why, though don't make that information a requirement for opting out. You can glean important insights this way, even from short responses. For example, you may be sending emails too frequently, or you may be focusing on products or services that don't reflect that customer's needs. Use this information to refine your email marketing campaign, keeping customer engagement high.

No matter how targeted your email marketing campaign might be, the information might never reach your ideal customers if you don't optimize your subject lines. According to Radicati Research Group, in 2014, most people received around 84 emails per day. Whether or not your email gets opened — or simply trashed — has everything to do with the subject line. One quick tip is to keep your subject lines under six words, which is the maximum length that appears seamlessly on a mobile device.

However, there is more to a strong subject line than brevity. Your subject lines also need to be engaging. If "March Newsletter" is your subject line, you're likely to miss the mark.

You should also take time to think about what device your ideal customers will use to read your emails. In 2014, according to Movable Ink, 66 percent of emails were opened on mobile devices, and that number is only going to rise, so your content and design must be mobile friendly.

Following these simple steps — to grow your email database, write engaging subject lines and design with mobile in mind — will have you well on your way to generating a strong return on your email-marketing investment.

GETTING SOPHISTICATED WITH EMAIL MARKETING

MEASUREMENT IS BECOMING an imperative in marketing. Savvy marketers naturally prefer to invest money in a strategy with a measurable return on investment, because without measurement, you're just throwing darts blindfolded. This is why email-marketing campaigns have remained so popular: it's easy to measure their effects and test out tweaks to generate stronger results.

Every marketer knows the importance of developing a growing list of email addresses, writing engaging subject lines, and keeping messages readable on mobile devices — but once you've mastered these basics of email marketing campaigns, you're ready to take some more complex tactics for a spin.

Professional email platforms have offered "trigger" capabilities for the last few years, allowing you to automatically and easily send lightly personalized emails to customers based on specific events. For example, you might send a traditional "welcome" message immediately after a new subscriber signs up for your newsletter or a "thank you" message after a customer places an order. However, now there are more sophisticated triggers worth taking for a spin.

For example, 30 days after your customers make purchases, you could automatically send an email prompting them to write reviews. You could also recommend additional products or services that complement their last purchases.

If the customer provided an email address to download an informative article or industry research, trigger an email offering related content to continue the conversation after the initial download. You should also send emails to prospects automatically when they move into a new step in the sales process. For example, you could send an FAQ addressing common customer concerns at each stage in your sales cycle, like describing how your product or service compares to the competition.

Today's consumers rely heavily on "social proof" before making purchases. They want to know what other consumers have to say about your brand. You can expedite your sales cycle by including customer reviews or positive customer tweets in your email campaigns.

You should also ensure that your campaigns each have a single call to action, asking the customer to take one specific next step. If you include more than one next step in your message, it can cause indecision, delayed responses or just generally lower response rates.

Email marketing is one of the easiest of all marketing channels to test and tweak. Start by dividing your audience in half, and test out two different emails. You could compare the results of two different subject lines, two headlines, two different days of the week or times of day for distribution, or sending the email from two different email addresses. In fact, the ease with which you can test one email marketing technique against another allows you to strategically break all the rules, one at a time, so you can determine what works uniquely for your brand.

FOUR STEPS TO GROW YOUR PROSPECT EMAIL LIST

ONE OF THE MOST cost-efficient strategies for driving website traffic and generating online leads is email marketing. Unfortunately, most small and mid-sized businesses only have the email addresses of current clients, business partners and other friends of the company.

If you're going to light a fire under your email marketing campaigns and dramatically boost results, you'll need to follow these four steps for growing your list of email addresses.

Begin your efforts by creating a reason to entice potential customers to give you their email addresses. What original content do you already offer your current customers? Consider informative white papers, webinars, podcasts, case studies, articles, research and industry tools, as well as videos of training, presentations or keynote addresses you've delivered.

Next, create a simple landing page for each piece of original content. Keep these pages easy to understand, with just a simple image, and a short contact form. Make sure you also provide a quick teaser of the content to entice each visitor to subscribe, but don't provide so much information that the visitor won't feel the need to download the content. On your contact form, explain that visitors can download the content for free, but only if they provide their email addresses. Keep in mind that requiring less information will drive higher participation levels. As such, make the visitor's name and email address the only required fields on this contact form. You can always make the visitor's company, title and phone number optional.

Work to convert your existing website traffic into email subscriptions by finding appropriate places on your website to promote your content offerings, like a blog, your resources page or even on your homepage. Design visually appealing banner ads that link to your free content. Organize all of your content into a resource center or library on your website that can serve as an ongoing source of website traffic, email subscribers and new customers.

Finally, promote your free content offerings through all of your active social media networks. LinkedIn is a particularly valuable network for this kind of promotion. Use your company page to promote this content, but leverage your personal network, too. If you're a member of relevant LinkedIn groups, promote your content offerings through those groups as well. Emphasize the value you're offering the group by giving away one piece of content on the social network itself, then promote a second piece of content with a link that requires contact information in order to begin the download.

Most companies these days are already investing time in developing original content. Why not get more value out of your content by repurposing it, and gaining the coveted email addresses of your ideal prospects in the process?

PSYCHOLOGY BEHIND SOCIAL MEDIA

A BRAND LEVERAGING SOCIAL MEDIA as an arrow in its quiver of marketing tools needs to know what drives people to engage with its brand. This has become the most important question of all, since mainstream social media sites like Facebook are placing increasing emphasis on how much your followers engage with your brand, instead of your total follower count.

According to a 2013 Stanford Study, conducted in collaboration with Facebook scientists, just 28 to 35 percent of those who have "liked" a brand's page are likely to see that brand's posts. That's because Facebook's algorithms filter content, prioritizing the posts from the people and brands users engage with most in their newsfeeds. If the users liking your page don't engage with your brand, the time you spend on content development could be a wasted effort, since your followers still may not be likely to see your content in their newsfeeds. And these viewership numbers have no doubt dropped since this study was conducted, as Facebook continues to limit "organic reach" in order to drive advertising revenue.

To deliver content that drives engagement, begin by understanding why people share posts.

A 2014 *New York Times* Customer Insight Group Survey uncovered the primary reasons people share or engage with social media content. Above all else, people share to bring valuable and entertaining content to others. They also like to get the word out about causes they are passionate about. Social sharing is an extension of relationship building for many people, with a large percentage using social-media communication as a way to define themselves to others and feel more involved in the world.

There are also a number of deep-seated psychological principles at play, like the rule of reciprocity. We naturally feel compelled to help those who have done something kind for us. If a brand shares your content, you may feel compelled to share that brand's material in return.

People are much more likely to believe content shared by several peers, rather than promotional content delivered directly by your brand. Consumers are also more likely to choose a brand with strong visibility and likability, instead of a company they haven't heard much about. When consumers see others, especially people they know and trust, engaging with your brand regularly on social media, their trust in your brand will increase, even without direct contact.

People also have an innate fear of missing out. In fact, most social media users believe they'll miss out on news, updates or events if they don't regularly check their networks. If you can position your brand as an authoritative, consistent source of credible news and thought leadership, people will rely on your brand as a trusted reference, engaging with you time and time again.

Understanding psychological needs of customers can help you refine your social media content so that it encourages two-way communication, which is what social media is all about.

Due to the dynamic nature of social media, this content may vary from evolved best practices.

INVESTING IN THE RIGHT SOCIAL MEDIA NETWORK

MORE THAN HALF OF BUSINESSES using social media marketing for more than three years reported an increase in sales over that time period, according to the 2012 Social Media Industry Report, but achieving these results requires a significant time investment, making it crucial to focus your social media marketing efforts on the right social networks.

How do you know which social media networks are right for your company? Begin by thinking about your goals. Do you want to reach new markets, grow sales from existing customers or monitor your brand's reputation online? Defining what success means to your company will help you narrow down where to start.

Once you know what you want to get out of your social media strategy, identify the social media networks where your target audiences are spending their time. You can ensure you're getting the most out of your investment in social media marketing by targeting your efforts toward one or two of the major social media platforms that have critical mass among your targeted prospects.

Still having trouble deciding? On the following page, you will find high-level overviews of the benefits and drawbacks of each of the major social media networks that may help influence your decision.

As of 2015, Facebook reported that it had more than 1.44 billion active users, which gives Facebook critical mass. And according to a 2015 SproutSocial article, 66 percent of men use Facebook, compared to 77 percent of women who use it. Average household income of Facebook users is greater than $70,000.

Facebook is viewed as a community, which means followers aren't likely to respond well to content that's directly promotional. On the other hand, Facebook offers the unique ability to engage in meaningful dialogue with your customers to enhance brand loyalty. Facebook allows for greater depth of engagement with your customers.

Twitter reports more than 302 million active users as of 2015, and while gaining ground on rival Facebook, it still has much ground to clear. The average Twitter user is 37 years old, and 64 percent of users are female, according to Media Bistro. AdWeek reported in 2015 that average household income for Twitter users was $79,000.

On Twitter, each post is limited to 140 characters, which makes it more challenging to build deep relationships with customers, but it can be a highly effective tool for sharing new blog posts, special offers and news about your company. Using hashtags by placing the pound sign in front of keywords allows your content to be discovered by users who might not have otherwise followed your brand. Because of hashtags, Twitter is a great way to reach individuals who may not already be familiar with your products and services.

LinkedIn has more than 364 million users according to its newsroom in 2015, and it has become the online destination for professionals to network. LinkedIn's highly educated users generate a household income of more than $87,000 on average, according to AdWeek. More than 60 percent of LinkedIn users are male, with an average age of 44.

Use this information to deliberately focus on developing your brand's presence on the social media network that's best for you and your company.

Due to the dynamic nature of social media, this content may vary from evolved best practices.

SOCIAL MEDIA: BEST OF THE REST

THERE ARE EASILY MORE THAN 20 significant social media networks available in 2015, and hundreds if you count the small and niche players, so it's easy to get overwhelmed with all of the choices available. Given the considerable amount of time that businesses are investing in social media marketing, it's vital to focus those efforts on the right networks versus diluting your efforts across too many. Even though Facebook, Twitter and LinkedIn are the three social media giants, there are certainly other contenders to consider.

For example, there's YouTube. YouTube isn't just for videos anymore. YouTube is a video search engine that offers social features as well. More than 1 billion unique users visit YouTube each month, per the YouTube website, and 40 to 50 percent of them are under the age of 35. According to Nielsen in 2014, YouTube reached more U.S. adults in the 18-34 age range than any cable network. The gender split is nearly even, with women making up 53 percent of users.

Google+ is another strong contender. The greatest benefit to this social network is that it is owned by Google, so it's easy to search — which means your posting efforts can improve your company's search results. Quickly outpacing Twitter, Google+ had roughly 540 million active users as of 2015, according to its website. Seventy-three percent of those users are male, making it the most male-oriented of the major social networks. ZogDigital, in 2014, reported that the average user age was 28.

Photo-sharing network Instagram has over 300 million active users, according to its website. Over 90 percent of users are under the age of 35, making it an ideal platform for brands targeting 18 to 34 year olds. Nearly 68 percent of Instagram's users are female.

Pinterest is a social network based on sharing images. What are Pinterest's 47 million active users, according to eMarketer in 2015, sharing? Food and drink-related images account for 18 percent of all items shared on Pinterest. Over 70 percent of Pinterest users are female. Retailers are given a particular advantage, in that Pinterest has an e-commerce element to it, allowing users to "pin" items they would like to buy and click through to those websites to make a purchase if they are so inclined. Most users access Pinterest through a tablet or other mobile device.

The options for promoting your brand on social media networks are endless, so you should ensure that you're making the most of your time investment by choosing the platform that best fits your business and attracts your targeted demographic. For example, if you are targeting professional women, Instagram or Pinterest might make more sense for your business than LinkedIn, since more than 60 percent of LinkedIn users are male. If you're targeting young adults, YouTube videos could reach your audience more effectively.

When it comes to social media marketing, now more than ever, you have to know your audience.

Due to the dynamic nature of social media, this content may vary from evolved best practices.

UNLEASHING AN ARMY OF BRAND AMBASSADORS

A STUDY BY LINKEDIN and research firm TNS in 2014 confirmed that 81 percent of small businesses use social media, but a much smaller percentage of those companies have figured out what roles their employees will play in their social media strategies.

Whether they know it or not, your employees play a part in your company's social media strategy. After all, it's likely that they are already regularly involved in social media — and since they spend more time working than engaging in any other activity, there's a high likelihood they occasionally mention their job online. So, while they may not be attending your social media strategy meetings, they are definitely influencing the outcome of those strategies.

Of course, paying your employees' paychecks doesn't entitle you to control what they do or say away from work, so avoid putting a heavy-handed social media policy in place. Instead, engage your employees in a dialogue about the role social media plays in building the company brand and how they can help. If you're persuasive, you can create a veritable army of brand ambassadors.

There are passive and active roles your employees can play in your company's social media strategy through their own personal profiles on sites like Facebook, Twitter and LinkedIn — but active participation requires more training and coaching. Clearly defining your employees' roles in your social media strategy can maximize their effectiveness.

There are four key roles they could play.

The Messenger is responsible for publishing messages about your company, whether that means formal press releases, blog posts, newsletters or more informal commentary on your team's current work. The mere act of talking about what you do reminds prospects and customers about your core competencies, as well as the depths of your product and service offerings. Messengers can be in primary roles by generating content, or they can play secondary roles, reposting the content generated by others.

The Scout is responsible for listening to commentary about your brand. Scouts scour social media sites looking for your company name and key words related to your business to learn what is being said, then sharing those findings with management. Some scouting parameters might include your company name, the names of your management team, and your competitors' names.

The Spokesperson is anyone who's responsible for responding to online commentary for your brand. You might have several employees in this role, but these employees need to be coached on the tone of your brand personality and how to navigate tricky issues.

The Sales Agent rides the social media wave, looking for prospective customers who are talking about your industry. If you run an HVAC company, for example, your Sales Agent would search Twitter for people in your market asking for recommendations for an air-conditioning repair. The Sales Agent would recommend your company and connect that person with a customer service team member.

Because your company's social media presence needs to be authentic, encourage employees to assume the roles they feel most comfortable with. Remember to acknowledge and reward employees who invest time and creativity in your company's social media strategy — possibly with an invitation to the next strategy meeting.

Due to the dynamic nature of social media, this content may vary from evolved best practices.

FROM MONOLOGUE TO DIALOGUE

YOU CAN NO LONGER count on traditional advertising alone to interrupt consumers and capture attention. There is simply too much advertising noise, and consumers can very easily turn it off for self-preservation. For example, DVRs allow your audience to skip TV commercials altogether, and when passengers are preoccupied on their smartphones, even billboards don't guarantee visibility. It's not an easy task to reach consumers when they have so many opportunities to easily disengage.

American Express chief marketing officer John Hayes summarized this shift clearly when he said, "We went from a monologue to a dialogue. Mass media will continue to play a role. But its role has changed." For more than a decade, the best companies have slowly shifted their focus in response, embracing social media networks and integrating print and TV campaigns with their online presence. Unfortunately, that's not enough.

Why? Consumers have become increasingly sensitive to the feeling of manipulation. If they believe you are using them only for your own benefit, consumers are quick to walk away. Price-driven, hypercritical consumers have been empowered, and they are turning to social media and online review sites for feedback about the brands they're considering. Instead of trusting your traditional marketing, consumers have begun to place their trust in other consumers, even if they don't know them. These online communications serve as your front-line sales team, and in fact, most of your consumers now are highly educated about your brand before they ever speak to you.

Once these consumers have reached out to your brand, how can you make the right impression and motivate consumers to continue to connect with your brand? When consumers make contact with your company, they're seeking true one-on-one engagement — not a barrage of one-way marketing messages.

Consumers want brands to talk with them, not at them; so companies of the future are embracing the fact that everyone in the organization is responsible for marketing. If you are going to truly connect with customers, all of your email messages, phone calls, social media posts, website content and even the in-store dialogue you have with customers have to leave the customer feeling as though you've delivered on your brand experience.

Because of the demands of these modern consumers, a much broader cross-section of your staff needs to be coached in the art of consumer engagement, and some will need specific training in the art of digital and social media marketing.

Marketing can no longer be handled in isolation by a single department. In this new era of consumer engagement, every employee who has contact with your customers in any way counts as a member of your marketing team, so it's crucial that your whole team understands and promotes the products, services and experiences your brand is promising consumers.

Due to the dynamic nature of social media, this content may vary from evolved best practices.

SEVEN SOCIAL MEDIA MISSTEPS TO AVOID

SOCIAL MEDIA can be an effective marketing channel with a relatively low hard cost. Once you consider your compensation per hour multiplied by the number of hours you and your team spend on social media each year, though, you will see why it's important to ensure you are getting a return on that significant time investment.

Start by avoiding these common missteps.

Not having a social media strategy in place will keep your company from seeing results. Begin developing your strategy by defining your target audiences, then research the demographics of the top social platforms to find out which networks are the best bets for your company. For example, Pinterest could be ideal for retailers looking to showcase new fashion or home interior products targeting women.

Posting too little or too much is another common misstep. While you don't want your social media profiles to resemble an online ghost town, with weeks between posts, it is also possible to post too often, which might cause followers to view your content as spam. While ideal post frequency can vary widely by industry and content type, a general rule of thumb is to post two times each week on LinkedIn, once daily on Facebook, and a minimum of three times each day on Twitter.

Not tracking the impact of your social media strategy can also hinder your results. Facebook, Twitter and LinkedIn all have strong analytic programs for monitoring your follower growth and levels of engagement. Combine this data with the number of visits to your website generated from your social channels and the resulting impact on your online sales, and you will begin to see the complete picture.

Focusing too much on promotional content should also raise a red flag. Use a 5 to 1 ratio: at least five posts that offer real value to your followers, like educational content or special offers available only to social media followers, for every one promotional post.

Not actually engaging with your audience is a huge pitfall as well. It's called social media because the intent is to be social, encouraging two-way conversations. Make time to listen and converse directly with your audience.

If you focus on quantity instead of quality of followers, your social media strategy will suffer. The size of your audience has very little to do with its value to your company. Focus on growing your customer base organically by cultivating messages for consumers who are truly interested in your content. These are your ideal audiences; don't neglect them just to search out a larger number of followers.

Posting the exact same messages across all of your networks, at the same time will bore your followers, because there's always a percentage of your customer base that follows you across multiple social networks. Mix it up, or else they might start tuning you out.

Due to the dynamic nature of social media, this content may vary from evolved best practices.

FACEBOOK MARKETING STRATEGIES

FACEBOOK IS A PLATFORM that has more than 1.44 billion monthly active users, as of early 2015, that can be accessed for free — in theory. It seems like a no-brainer for businesses to have a presence there.

Having a business page on Facebook is easy. Anyone can create a page fairly easily — but just because you build it, doesn't mean that they will come. Facebook requires a fairly hefty time investment from your company in order to leverage your company's page to its full potential. And while Facebook is theoretically free for everyone, brands are rather universally concerned about the fact that Facebook's algorithms make it difficult for their status updates to be seen by fans organically.

Just because someone likes your business page doesn't mean your status updates will appear in that person's newsfeed. However, Facebook will place an ad in front of your fans — for a fee, of course.

If used effectively, well-timed, highly targeted Facebook ads can drive more business to your page or website and produce a significant return on your investment, but don't get tricked by the idea that all follower growth is worth the investment. Not all "likes" are created equally. An artificially inflated follower count might look nice, but if those followers don't fall within your target audience and aren't genuinely interested in your brand, they won't interact with you or make a purchase, making them essentially worthless. So focus your Facebook advertising on users that align with your target.

You can also grow your follower base organically. One of the simplest ways is to post content on your page that authentically engages real fans. Ask them questions, hold contests and post photos or interesting videos that will inspire your followers to engage. The more your followers engage with you, the more often your updates will appear in their Facebook newsfeeds and those of their friends, encouraging additional like-minded followers.

Don't ask questions or hold contests at random, though. Use the Insights analytics feature on Facebook to determine when your fans are online. Remember that posting when your followers are active doesn't necessarily mean you have to be on Facebook at that time, since Facebook allows you to schedule posts in advance.

Make sure that you interact with your followers who take the time to stop by and comment. Make them feel like they are part of the community with personalized responses.

Another way to drive more traffic to your Facebook page is to leverage your brand's website with a well-placed social media icon on each page. Remember to include all of your social media links or handles on business cards, packaging, store signs and email signatures, too. Make it easy for your fans to find you.

Due to the dynamic nature of social media, this content may vary from evolved best practices.

TWITTER MARKETING STRATEGIES

A FRIEND OF MINE told an interesting story recently. He was considering hiring a lawn care service, and his eye was on a particular company, but that company's competitor offered him $10 off each of his first five applications. Luke was now also considering the competitor.

My friend is actually a complete stranger who "told" this story on Twitter. In one 140-character tweet, Luke wrote how he had mentioned the first company in a previous tweet, and shared how the previously unknown competitor — having read this tweet — subsequently offered him $10 off.

Luke shows how consumers are using Twitter with brand mentions, and how those brands can best use the platform to target prospective customers.

Clearly, whoever is running the Twitter account at the second lawn care business is keeping up with the mentions of its competitors. Tweeting to consumers talking about your competitors gets your brand name into the consciousness of prospects when they are likely to be very close to the point of purchase.

That's just smart marketing, and it is one effective way brands can leverage Twitter.

In a world of a decreasing attention span, Twitter allows users to scroll through the noise, one 140-character tweet at a time. If you want to use Twitter for marketing, keep these strategies in mind as you define your plan.

Separate your personal and business accounts. If you have one personal Twitter account and another for your brand profile, ensure the content is different or your followers may begin to tune one of them out — or maybe even both. It's okay to retweet your brand content from your personal profile, though.

Double-check your hashtags. Used to create conversations around trending topics, hashtags are a great way to get your message seen by people who don't follow you directly, but before you use a hashtag, make sure you understand how it's being used already by the Twitter community, so you can judge whether or not it matches your company's mission and your true communication objectives.

Don't trust automation exclusively. Many businesses and individuals use automation enablers such as Buffer or Hootsuite to schedule tweets in advance. However, in this case, you don't want to "set it and forget it." What might seem like an innocent tweet at the time can become inflammatory or insensitive depending on world events occurring in the moment, even if those events are out of your control.

Remember, too, that you don't need to participate in every trend. Putting your own spin on a trend in pop culture can backfire. Don't try to spin negative trends into a "clever" pitch. Instead of seeming trendy, you could end up sounding tone-deaf.

Finally, adopt the philosophy that when in doubt, you should leave it out. If you're at all concerned about how a tweet may be interpreted, don't risk it.

Due to the dynamic nature of social media, this content may vary from evolved best practices.

SEVEN TWITTER TIPS YOU MAY BE MISSING

MOST BUSINESSES have Twitter profiles, but very few are satisfied with the outcome of their Twitter strategies. Leverage these seven Twitter "tricks of the trade" to ensure you're getting the most of your time investment.

First, make sure you have enough of the right followers. Find businesses similar to yours in your market with similar target audiences, and begin following the people who follow them. Many of those people will follow you back either to reciprocate or because they have an interest in your industry.

Conduct an advanced search for followers at http://search.twitter.com. You can search for tweets referencing keywords that might interest your targeted followers. For example, try using examples like "intellectual property" for law firms or "designer shoes" for a shoe boutique. You can filter your search on proximity to your city, which is handy for businesses that only market themselves locally or regionally. Once you've identified a targeted list, follow those users, and a number of them are likely to follow you back.

One word of advice, though: Before your following spree, ensure your most recent post is relevant to new followers. If you have a frozen yogurt shop, for example, you might tweet, "Always on the search for other Memphis people on Twitter who love frozen treats."

As you grow your follower base, nurture those followers and engage them. Focus on at least two per day that you'll make a concerted effort to engage with.

Advertising your Twitter handle can also boost qualified followers. Include your company Twitter handle on your website, business cards, email signature, LinkedIn profile and email campaign stationery. Leverage your website to call even more attention to your Twitter profile by publishing a real-time feed of your tweets on your home page.

To engage and retain followers, create value through your content. Offer followers exclusive content or discounts not available elsewhere. Hold Twitter contests with a grand-prize winner and where everyone who participates gets a discount for answering a trivia question, for example, or retweeting a specific message.

With all of the social media platforms that we have to maintain these days, it's critical to be efficient at posting content. Consider writing your content in batches, at least a week at a time, then publishing those tweets at scheduled times throughout the week by using tools like Buffer, Sprout Social or HootSuite. These tools also allow you to post messages across several of your social media accounts within one convenient application.

There's a lot more to Twitter than simply posting updates about your day. If you're ready to get serious, test some of these strategies, measure your results, and then refine your strategy accordingly. Happy tweeting.

Due to the dynamic nature of social media, this content may vary from evolved best practices.

TOP TWITTER TURNOFFS

TWITTER USERS OFTEN make a split-second decision about whether or not to follow you, which means you have to make a positive first impression to gain new followers.

While some prospective followers may click to see your full profile, the lion's share make their determinations based solely on your summary screen — your personal avatar, the background image you've selected, your bio, your location, the Web address you choose to promote and your statistics.

Featured statistics include the number of tweets you've made since creating the profile, the number of Twitter users you're following, and the number following you. Since this is all most users will ever see about you before deciding whether you are "follow-worthy," make each element count — and be sure to avoid these top Twitter turnoffs.

One of the fastest ways to turn off a potential follower is by not uploading a photo or brand logo for your avatar, which leaves the default Twitter "egg" as your image. Users want to get a quick snapshot of your brand personality when viewing your profile. Since your avatar is so small, be sure the photo or image used is clearly visible, even on a small mobile screen.

Are you an over-tweeter? If you created your brand profile in 2006 when Twitter was launched, and tweeted five times a day over the next ten years, you would have sent about 18,000 tweets. If your count is more like 100,000, some followers may not follow you because they fear you'll clog up their feeds. In contrast, if you've sent only 20 tweets and are following thousands, you might be viewed as a social stalker.

Twitter will display a few of your recent tweets on your summary profile. If you seem to have an automated service tweeting on your behalf, or if you're only retweeting others, you're less likely to get followed.

If you have a third-party program set up to automatically send a promotional direct message to any new follower, there's a good chance you're going to get unfollowed fast. No one likes spam. Even an auto message that thanks someone for following you and encourages that person to visit your website is promotional, and many people would consider it inappropriate.

Your bio can only be four lines long, so it needs to pack a punch and show your personality. If your bio is boring, people will have trouble imagining that your tweets have much more to offer.

Finally, if the number of people you follow is significantly higher than the number following you, your profile may look like a spam account. If you're new to Twitter, pace yourself and resist the temptation to over-follow before you create a decent following of your own.

Due to the dynamic nature of social media, this content may vary from evolved best practices.

ENGAGING FOLLOWERS VIA LINKEDIN COMPANY PAGE

LINKEDIN, THE WORLD'S LARGEST social media platform specifically targeting the business community, has grown to roughly 350 million users in 2015 according to Statista. And businesses have taken note, with more than four million of them flocking to create company pages in order to tap into this critical mass of business professionals.

If you have a company page, follow these best practices to drive brand loyalty and generate qualified leads — ensuring you get the most out of your time investment.

Establish a strong presence by crafting a compelling and search-friendly company description, leading quickly with impactful, keyword-rich copy.

Attract followers by producing compelling content of interest to your target market. Post an update at least once per day by identifying regular contributors and creating a content calendar. Make content go further by breaking up lengthy material into a series, encouraging readers to regularly tune in. Avoid being too "sales-y" with your updates, making sure each update offers real value to followers.

Links and questions drive engagement. Updates containing a link are reported by LinkedIn to drive 45 percent higher engagement levels than those without, with those featuring questions (e.g., about industry trends or new products) driving 50 percent higher engagement.

Share relevant content found outside of LinkedIn, such as the results of third-party research, customer satisfaction scores, customer comments on a recent blog post, or feedback by customers captured through your call center.

Target your updates to particular audiences. If you have followers all across the world, but plan to post content about a local event you're hosting, you can target that content to your local footprint. Other targeting options include: company size, industry, function and seniority.

Embed "like" and "share" plug-ins within your website to encourage LinkedIn users to easily share content from your website with their network or to simply notify their connections that they like a product or service featured on your site.

Actively participate in groups comprised of your targeted prospects. Contribute to popular discussions, establishing yourself as a subject-matter expert. Where appropriate, link to your company page or website with additional information you deem helpful to those in the group.

Monitor LinkedIn analytics regularly to determine the best time to post your content, though generally morning updates generate the strongest engage-ment, followed by shortly after the workday. Also measure the engagement rate for your company page overall, as well as specific updates.

Engagement is the ratio of clicks, likes, comments and shares to total impres-sions, which helps you understand what content is resonating most strongly with your followers.

Your conversion rate is the ultimate best practice in tracking your LinkedIn company page performance, as it measures how successful your LinkedIn company page has been at driving qualified leads into your organization.

Due to the dynamic nature of social media, this content may vary from evolved best practices.

TO BLOG OR NOT TO BLOG?

TO BLOG OR NOT TO BLOG? Though certainly not as life or death as Shakespeare's original version, it's an interesting question faced by countless business owners and marketing professionals every day. Business blogs often feature commentary by management, product updates, upcoming events, or recent news about the company.

Few people have the capacity to regularly invest in creating original content for a blog without eventually seeing a measurable result on the business, but many businesses jump into blogging without first establishing realistic objectives and an understanding about how to execute an effective blog strategy. That's why 95 percent of blogs fail, and are eventually abandoned by their developers. Before committing to a blog, be clear on what it can and can't do for your business.

If you're a small business and can't cost justify the price of a professionally designed website, a blog can be a low-cost alternative.

If you do have a strong web presence but your site wasn't built with a content management tool that allows you to easily make updates, consider adding a blog. It allows a non-tech person to easily post content updates without the time and expense of paying a web developer to do so. However, content on a blog is generally more difficult for a website visitor to find than if it were placed directly on your website, so drive traffic to it by posting teasers on Twitter or Facebook with links to your blog.

Perhaps the greatest benefit of a blog is search engine optimization (SEO). It's the process of improving your website's ranking with the search engines through organic methods, rather than buying guaranteed search-engine placement through search-engine marketing.

Google makes no secret that it favors "quality content" over "self promotion," so current commentary found on blogs and social media sites carry more weight than the promotional content written for your website.

Small to mid-sized businesses often struggle to generate strong Google rankings due to the limited volume of content on their sites. Consistently updating a blog can significantly increase the amount of content Google can find. More posts mean that you have a higher page count on your site, creating a stronger likelihood that relevant keywords are included. This can lead to a higher ranking in Google search results for your business.

However, unless you have a particularly interesting perspective on a popular topic, along with the writing skills to engage your audience, flocks of readers aren't likely to regularly visit your blog.

The average Internet user visits a handful of blogs per month, and you're competing with giants like Mashable. Focus instead on driving search traffic to your blog and improving your search-engine ranking. Even if your blog doesn't lead to a regular following, you're still likely to see results from your blog strategy.

Due to the dynamic nature of social media, this content may vary from evolved best practices.

FIVE BEST PRACTICES FOR LEVERAGING PINTEREST

VIRTUAL SCRAPBOOKING SITE Pinterest has quickly taken the world of social media by storm, leaving some business owners and marketers scratching their heads about how exactly to leverage this social network. To avoid spinning your wheels, use these tips to make sure you're getting the most out of your time investment.

On Pinterest, users cultivate collections of images by "pinning" — or saving — the images they like best to their own "pinboards." Most brands use Pinterest as a springboard for driving traffic to their websites. Being able to link to other online content makes Pinterest a viable marketing tool for retailers with interesting, visual products — especially those conducive to consumer impulse-buying. With more than 53 million monthly visitors, Pinterest provides more referral traffic to other sites than Google+, YouTube and LinkedIn combined, according to a 2014 study by Shareaholic Reports.

Because Pinterest is based on images, the images your company provides need to be visually interesting. Pinterest isn't the site for everyday predictable photography, so pin beautiful photos of your products if you want Pinterest users to take interest. If your products aren't visually engaging themselves, consider a possible entertainment angle that communicates what you do while demonstrating that your team doesn't take itself too seriously.

You can also pin photos that offer your customers new ideas for how your products can be used. Handmade and vintage goods retailer, Etsy, shows consumers how they can incorporate the company's vintage products into their everyday lives by showcasing products on Pinterest in an at-home setting. This retailer has racked up nearly 600,000 Pinterest followers as a result, as of mid-year 2015.

Comment, repin and like the posts of those you follow and that follow you. After all, it is called "social" media for a reason. Start a conversation. Remember that conversations lead to relationships, which can lead to sales — but be careful not to hard sell your followers, or else they might revolt.

Consider unexpected themes for your pin boards. Neiman Marcus organizes its pins into boards called "Hello Sunshine," "The Art of Red" or "Make Some Noise," instead of using the expected "new products" board that so many retailers offer. Get creative. Pinterest users are inspired by innovative thinking.

Integrate Pinterest into your website by offering your website visitors a link to your Pinterest page on your website home page as well as a Pinterest icon on each of your product pages, allowing site visitors to easily share your product photos on their boards.

Pinterest's increasing popularity among retailers demonstrates the increasingly large role that social-media platforms play in the marketing world. Use these Pinterest tips to showcase your brand's creativity, which should, in turn, ensure your time is well spent.

Due to the dynamic nature of social media, this content may vary from evolved best practices.

TEN WAYS TO ATTRACT PINTEREST FOLLOWERS

PINTEREST REACHED 47 MILLION active users in 2015 according to eMarketer. If you're new to Pinterest, it's a virtual scrapbooking site that allows users to "pin" images they like and share those pins with friends. It's akin to online window-shopping, with the option to flag and organize photos of items you like for later viewing. These images are often linked to online content, such as product websites, making Pinterest a viable marketing tool for retailers with interesting, visual products generally conducive to impulse-buying.

At the beginning, Pinterest's user base was dominated by female consumers, who still make up about 70 percent of users, according to Sprout Social in 2015. Next came the big brands. Also according to Sprout Social, recent studies estimate that about 60 percent of the world's top brands have Pinterest accounts.

According to USA Today, Pinterest has its sights set on the small-business market now, with many small businesses keenly aware that most "pinners" are in shopping mode while on the site, and they're open to making purchases. As with most social media sites, you need followers for pinning to be worth your effort — but your total number of followers is less important than the number of followers in your target market, since they're the most likely to make a purchase.

Follow these ten tips to gather more followers for your brand's Pinterest page.

1. Pin regularly — at least five to 10 times a day, depending on the number of active boards you maintain.

2. A 2015 Sprout Social article says product pins featuring pricing in the description are 36 percent more apt to be "liked."

3. Add meaningful comments to popular pins, but focus on pins that relate to your market.

4. Include a link to your Pinterest account in your other social-media bios, on your website and in your email signature.

5. Place your most popular boards in the top row of your Pinterest page.

6. Contribute quality pins to group boards with a lot of followers.

7. Follow pinners with a large following of their own, especially if they follow boards related to your business category. Generally, about 20 percent will follow you in return.

8. Pin newsworthy content so you're seen as a thought leader. Be one of the first to create pins for news items or new product releases in your industry. And try to pin original content versus repinning.

9. Use search-friendly keywords when writing captions for your pins so they are likely to show up in relevant searches. Avoid a laundry list of keywords; instead, work them into your captions in a meaningful way.

10. Follow individuals who follow your competitors, since they are likely to be interested in your contributions as well.

By using these ten tips, you'll be able to quickly build a well-targeted, engaged Pinterest following.

Due to the dynamic nature of social media, this content may vary from evolved best practices.

INSTAGRAM MARKETING SECRETS

IT'S NOT OFTEN that a company with essentially no revenue sells for nearly a billion dollars, but that's what happened when Facebook wrote the largest check in history for a social-media network in 2012. What inspired Facebook's record-breaking purchase of Instagram?

Instagram is a photo-sharing program. It allows users to take and retouch photos, using a variety of interesting effects, like applying futuristic or retro filters. It also allows users to share these photos with others on Instagram, Facebook and Twitter. Instagram users can "like" and comment on one another's photos, similar to the way people interact on Facebook.

As of March 2015, Statista.com reports that Instagram has more than 300 million users. It's an impressive stat for a 2010 start-up. Many believe that Facebook's founder was threatened by Instagram's growing user base and its degree of service overlap. After all, what Facebook users like most about the network is the ability to share photos. Instagram was designed for mobile use, so once Instagram began adding social-media messaging capabilities, they were attacking Facebook's weak spot, since Facebook's mobile app had been widely viewed over the years as mediocre.

More and more brands are developing an Instagram presence, but luxury brands like Starbucks, Burberry, Audi and Mercedes were the early adopters. For these brands, creating an emotional connection with buyers is the name of the game, and they know that sharing interesting images allows consumers to imagine how their lives might change as a result of their products.

If you're new to Instagram, get started by determining what your followers expect from your brand. What interests your customers most? Once you've found your niche, stick to it, but be careful not to overdo it. Most Instagram users follow fewer than 200 people. If you post 10 photos in a row, they might feel like you're hijacking their feeds. That's a great way to get "unfollowed."

Next, make sure you're using relevant hashtags. Due to Instagram's simplicity, advanced search features aren't available, so it's essential that you include relevant hashtags in your photo captions to allow new followers to find you and your photos.

If you're still not sure whether or not your brand is a good fit for Instagram, here's food for thought: Photos are twice as likely to be shared through social media than text links. If your brand lends itself to interesting photography and you're looking for greater consumer engagement with your brand, this network may well be worth your time.

Due to the dynamic nature of social media, this content may vary from evolved best practices.

MARKETING STRATEGIES ON VINE

GIVEN THE INCREASINGLY SHORTER attention span of today's Web user, it's no wonder Twitter's looping video app, Vine, is waltzing its way into brand marketing strategies across the globe. Since Vine gathered more than 40 million users just after its first year, it's giving Instagram a run for its money. More importantly, video-sharing platforms, like Vine, are expected to grow over the next several years. Video is the new frontier in driving higher levels of social-media engagement.

Vine enables users to post and share six-second looping video clips via their mobile devices. The camera records only while the screen is being touched, allowing for on-the-fly editing and stop-motion effects. Vine video clips can be shared to the Vine network, Twitter, Facebook or Tumblr. Vine allows your video content to go viral quickly and easily, as users can just click the "revine" button beneath your Vine video to instantly post it to their profiles for their followers to see.

While more business-to-consumer (B2C) brands are using Vine than their business-to-business (B2B) counterparts, participation by both groups is increasing significantly. To determine if Vine is right for your business, look at Vine's user demographics to ensure your target market is well represented.

According to a 2014 NuVoodoo Poll, the top age demographic for Vine is 18-34 year olds with 15 percent of them using the app.

If Vine is a fit for your brand, consider some of these strategies.

Make the process of receiving and un-boxing your products a fun one, by shooting videos that remind viewers of opening a present on Christmas morning.

Reveal new products by showing just half of the new product, asking your customers to guess what the new product might be. You could also show viewers how your product is made with a behind-the-scenes video, or solve problems that relate to the products or services you offer by posting ultra short how-to videos.

Tell the six-second version of your company history or commitment to giving back to the community.

Give a tour of your office, or ask customers for video testimonials that you can string together to share how customers see your brand.

Whether or not Vine makes sense for your brand, there's no denying the increasing importance of sharable video content for consumers.

Due to the dynamic nature of social media, this content may vary from evolved best practices.

REAL-TIME MARKETING

BECAUSE WE LIVE in a digital world, we've grown accustomed to real-time communication with one another — and with the brands we care about. Now, there is a growing expectation of real-time response from companies. Even small businesses need to become more nimble and proactive, communicating at the same pace as their customers.

Thankfully, real-time communication doesn't necessarily mean that your responses need be instantaneous, but it does mean you need to respond quickly enough to be relevant. Consider Oreo's response to the blackout during Super Bowl XLVII in 2013. Shortly after the Superdome fell dark, the Oreo brand tweeted "You can still dunk in the dark," which was retweeted 10,000 times in one hour.

If your real-time marketing strategies are going to be effective, you'll need to establish a framework to give your social-media managers the freedom to post on the fly. Clearly outline the types of content you consider appropriate to post, establish guidelines accordingly and then ensure your team is empowered to make real-time decisions off the cuff. Oreo's tweet went viral because the message was deployed within a few minutes of the blackout.

While it may sound counterintuitive, successful real-time marketing requires planning in advance. If you just shoot from the hip, you probably won't see strong results.

If you run an area restaurant, part of your real-time marketing planning may be deciding when you will focus on social media. If your lunch service has opportunity for growth, then you may focus on real-time social-media marketing tactics from 10:00 am until noon every day by watching users on popular social media platforms talking about their plans for lunch. If they're inquiring about where to eat or commenting about plans to visit a competing restaurant, message them real time with an invitation to visit your restaurant for special VIP treatment, like dining at the chef's table or trying out a new dessert for free.

It's more efficient to take your marketing to where your prospective buyers already are, instead of trying to entice them elsewhere to see your message. Similarly, in the social media arena, it is easier to engage consumers about topics that are already top of mind, like holidays, the Oscars or the Final Four.

For example, Universal Music once deployed an email campaign that was a perfect example of social-media marketing that reflected current events. The emails were sent right after the Olympics, making the music that was used in the Closing Ceremonies available for digital download. This strategy, called "Newsjacking," works well if your audience is interested in the event you're referencing — but only if you can find an authentic way to connect it to your business without seeming desperate.

The formula for a successful real-time marketing strategy is simple: establish guidelines, empower your team and determine where and when you're likely to generate the greatest response for your time investment.

Due to the dynamic nature of social media, this content may vary from evolved best practices.

ONLINE REPUTATION COULD BE KILLING YOUR BUSINESS

A WHOPPING 72 PERCENT of consumers globally report trusting online reviews from strangers when making purchase decisions, according to BrightLocal's 2014 Consumer Review Survey. In fact, four out of five consumers say they would reverse their purchasing decision based on negative online reviews, according to a 2011 Cone study of online trends.

If many of your other marketing efforts — like your social-media marketing, email campaigns and print ads — are ultimately designed to drive consumers to your website, you're likely to lose these customers to competitors with more savvy online skills if your online reputation is poor or nonexistent.

Once you've considered these facts, it becomes clear that online reputation management has never been more imperative.

Imagine this horrifying scenario: you've been delivering for your customers consistently for years, exceeding expectations. Unbeknownst to you, a former customer posts unfair reviews of your business online, creating a twisted sense of reality. Because you're not encouraging your current customers to post positive reviews, the only thing your prospective customers see are these negative comments, resulting in what could be significant loss of business.

The bottom line is that if you're not monitoring your brand's online reputation, a few negative reviews could kill your business.

The first step in online reputation management is monitoring. Set up a Google Alert notifying you every time someone mentions your brand online. This will catch some but not all customer reviews, as many review sites require log-in for entry, which prevents a Google Alert from detecting the mention.

Supplement this by putting a weekly reminder on your calendar to search for your company on the most relevant review sites for your business category. If you run a residential service company, Angie's List is important. For restaurants, Yelp and Urbanspoon are both crucial. You might also consider using a site like ReviewTrackers.com, which allows you to track your reviews from the major review sites in one convenient location for a fee.

Next, set up a system to encourage your customers to submit online reviews to a variety of sites. Never put all of your eggs in a single review site's basket, as you wouldn't want your company's future dictated by a single vendor with no vested interest.

You should aim to accumulate a sizeable quantity of recent, positive reviews from actual customers. Both consumers and search engines place greater value on newer reviews, which means you'll want to regularly ask your customers to review your company online. If you have two positive online reviews over the past year compared to a competitor with over 100, which company do you think consumers will gravitate toward naturally?

If you receive a negative review, remember not to panic. Respond to the customer publicly, and demonstrate your willingness to make it right with full transparency. Offer to take the conversation off line for full resolution. If you're running a sound company and proactively encouraging customers to review your brand online, the good will inevitably outweigh the occasional bad review.

Due to the dynamic nature of social media, this content may vary from evolved best practices.

GUERRILLA TACTICS - POWERFUL WEAPON IN CONSUMER WARFARE

GUERRILLA WARFARE IS, by definition, unconventional. It's where a small group of combatants use less structured, mobile tactics — like ambushes and raids — to combat a larger, more formal, less mobile army. Think rag-tag Americans shooting from trees at spit-polished British soldiers.

In the marketing world, guerrilla marketing has come to mean unconventional, less-structured marketing techniques that are often more easily deployed by small firms. It allows small companies to compete with the big dogs because small businesses are more agile and flexible. Even better, guerrilla marketing relies more heavily on ingenuity than a big financial investment. It's the great equalizer for small and mid-sized business owners.

The term "guerrilla marketing" was coined years ago by Jay Conrad Levinson in his book by the same name, and given recent economic realities, guerrilla marketing has never been more relevant.

Guerrilla tactics cut through all the messaging clutter competing for prospective customers' attention, and in a sea of advertising where true creativity is hard to come by, guerrilla marketing can help your brand stand out.

Some forms of guerrilla marketing tap into many of the five senses — getting people to see, touch, taste, hear or even smell a brand. Most importantly, guerrilla marketing is effective because it can create organic, word-of-mouth buzz that outlasts your campaign.

For example, in 2007, Nissan unleashed a relatively quiet but effective guerrilla marketing campaign that could have just as easily been launched on a smaller scale by a small-business owner.

To promote Nissan's new, at the time, technology that allowed an Altima owner to start the car by pressing a button on the dash rather than inserting a key, the company "lost" 20,000 sets of keys in concert halls, sports arenas and a variety of other public places in targeted cities.

Each key had a tag attached that read, "If found, please do not return. My Next Generation Nissan Altima has Intelligent Key with push-button ignition, and I no longer need these." The tag also encouraged readers to visit the Nissan website to learn more about this new technology.

The message was simple, and the campaign had a very modest cost for a company Nissan's size — but the buzz was extraordinary, and it lasted well past the expiration of the promotion.

So if your marketing needs a boost, you should think outside traditional advertising. What is your version of the "lost keys" campaign?

How can you sneak up on prospective customers and pleasantly surprise them?

GO BIG OR GO HOME

THERE'S A PHRASE I'VE USED over and over, throughout my years in marketing: "Go big or go home." It embodies my die-hard philosophy that marketing should stand out from the crowd, and that you have to be willing to take risks to get the most out of a limited marketing budget.

It is far better to be remembered for using a marketing message or communications channel that's interesting, funny, edgy or even a little risky, than to be forgotten because of lackluster "me-too" design and messaging.

Las Vegas is a city that makes it clear that they fully embrace the "go big or go home" concept, and a trip to Las Vegas reminded me of that. Standing at the airport's baggage carousel alongside hoards of other travelers, I waited for my luggage.

Our flight's luggage was late. Despite the fact that I had fully investigated the only piece of luggage moving past us — a nondescript black roller bag — at least 25 times, we still stood there staring at the carousel trying to will our luggage into existence. We were a captive audience to say the least.

Suddenly, I noticed a commotion moving like a wave around the luggage-belt; one traveler after another reacted. Then the cause of the commotion made its way around the corner to me. It was a small, red trunk with a pair of women's legs protruding from the side, as though she had been cut in half. The trunk was simply labeled "Lance Burton, Master Magician, Monte Carlo."

Like all big casinos, the Monte Carlo has a hefty marketing budget, especially compared to most small businesses — but even though mass media advertising, like network TV, is an option, the Monte Carlo chose to dedicate resources to guerrilla marketing in an effort to stand out from the crowd of other casinos vying for travelers' attention.

My guess is that this guerrilla marketing effort cost them only a few hundred dollars to execute, but generated an exponentially higher payoff. With a little ingenuity, "going big" doesn't have to equate to a big budget.

Sometimes the "go big or go home" philosophy means just sitting it out. One CEO of a small business recently told me about his intent to rent a trade show booth, but after the booth rental he wouldn't have money for a display and giveaways to compete with other exhibitors. My advice was to wait until next year, when he could "go big" and stand apart from competing exhibitors.

I recommended that he simply attend this year's event as a guest to network and conduct a little competitive espionage.

What will it be? Will your company go big, or will you go home?

Next time someone in your business has an unusual marketing idea, go ahead and laugh — but if you can find the resolve you need to try it, you might just discover some marketing magic.

MISS AMERICA AND THE MOONINITES

STUNT MARKETING ISN'T NEW. We could all learn a marketing lesson from the Miss America pageant, which debuted back in the 1920s as a stunt to draw tourists to Atlantic City after the high season. In 1903, newspaper publisher Henri Desgrange launched a bicycle race as a stunt to promote his paper. He never imagined the Tour de France would be going strong more than 100 years later. As you can see, when stunt marketing works, the buzz and publicity can last for years.

Can stunt marketing still work today? Consumer buying behaviors have fundamentally changed as a result of the exponential explosion of social media, so it's no surprise that there's more marketing messaging than ever competing for the attention of your customers online. Consumers now have little patience for searching out companies in the purposeful way they used to. Instead, they listen to their friends' social media commentary about brands and products.

The only way to break through this noise is to create a brand experience worthy of buzz: a truly memorable experience that motivates your target audience to like your brand, share their perspectives and tweet about you to their followers and friends. What better way to take a customer by surprise — creating a lasting, buzz-worthy memory — than through stunt marketing?

Passersby on a busy street corner in the Netherlands were shocked to see a severed arm lying on the sidewalk. Upon closer scrutiny, they noticed the gory movie prop was holding a copy of Death Proof, a movie written and directed by Tennessee native Quentin Tarantino, who is known for creating edgy films.

The buzz was global.

This stunt could have just as easily been executed by a small business. That's the beauty of guerrilla marketing. It allows small businesses to compete with much larger competitors because it relies more on creativity than cash.

Stunt marketing can also be dangerous, since missteps can be very public and equally costly. Cartoon Network learned that lesson the hard way in 2007 while promoting Aqua Teen Hunger Force, a mature cartoon with a cult following that always aired late at night during the network's Adult Swim programming line up.

The Cartoon Network placed 40 battery-powered LED placards — that resembled Mooninite characters from the cartoon when lit — across the city of Boston, mostly in high-traffic areas. However, they didn't plan for the "Lite-Brite" devices to be discovered during daylight hours.

While the niche of consumers targeted by this stunt marketing campaign eventually understood that they were looking at Mooninites once they saw the placards lit up, in our post-9/11 environment, the rest of the city was alarmed by mysterious electronic gadgets placed under bridges and around high-traffic areas. Bomb squads were called in. Major traffic corridors were completely shut down. The cost to the city, and ultimately to the network, was huge.

While we should all learn from the Cartoon Network's mistakes, by always vetting high-profile concepts with an objective audience, stunt marketing is still a powerful way to stretch a limited marketing budget. If you're working with limited marketing resources, consider a stunt marketing campaign to stand out from the crowd of competitors, engage prospective customers and illustrate your brand's unique personality.

AMBIENT MARKETING CREATES LASTING IMPRESSION

AMBIENT MARKETING is an underutilized form of guerrilla marketing that aims to catch the attention of prospective customers in nontraditional locations, where and when they are most open to considering your products or services.

Perhaps the most challenging aspect of ambient marketing is identifying nontraditional locations. After all, what's nontraditional today could be mainstream tomorrow. That's why this style of guerrilla marketing is underutilized. It requires a brand to regularly reinvent its marketing strategies. The most successful ambient campaigns are often in pervasive and ubiquitous environments, stopping the public in its tracks, and creating a lasting impression they feel compelled to share with others.

For example, Spar Restaurant in Mumbai deployed an ambient strategy to promote its seafood festival. The restaurant scattered realistic-looking, oversized plastic clamshells on the local beach. Consumers engaged with the campaign by opening the shells, finding a flier promoting the restaurant's seafood festival inside.

The campaign used an unexpected location, creatively engaged consumers and formed a memorable impression. Most importantly, the restaurant spoke to consumers at a time when they were likely most receptive to seafood, which is the real secret to ambient marketing.

The more you can involve your audience, the better. The more unusual the campaign, the more time the average consumer is willing to spend engaging with that campaign. Once consumers have invested that time to understand it, their openness to consider your products or services and tell others about their experience increases exponentially.

How consumers discover your campaign also impacts its effectiveness. When they feel like they've stumbled across it themselves, they are more likely to feel connected to your brand and tell others.

The American Red Cross launched a brilliantly simple ambient marketing campaign to encourage large numbers of new donors to make small donations — pocket change, in fact. The challenge was in determining how to best solicit people for their spare pocket change, ideally at a time when it's actually in their hands.

Since the typical donations box you see next to retail checkout stands across America are highly expected and easy to ignore, the Red Cross thought about the fact that travelers have their change out when passing through airport security. In partnership with an airport authority, the organization replaced the nondescript gray bins with brightly colored Red Cross branded versions featuring two compartments: a large section for the traveler's personal belongings and a smaller slot labeled, "Your change is welcome here. Donate it."

It was an easy request that didn't require travelers to think too hard before making a donation. The campaign was engaging, and the donation process was simple. Most importantly, the Red Cross targeted travelers at a time when they're already thinking about their pocket change.

In a marketplace where your prospective customers are flooded with more messages than they can possibly digest, connecting with your customers in their own backyards can pay big dividends.

POWER OF INFLUENCE

ACCORDING TO A 2013 NIELSEN STUDY, nearly 77 percent of people prefer to learn about products through word of mouth, and more than 90 percent of consumers would try a product or service if it was recommended to them by a friend.

Influencer marketing is a form of guerrilla marketing that focuses on persuading key individuals, instead of convincing the market as a whole. Usually, there are a few individuals that have a lot of sway over your prospective buyers. Influencer marketing strategies are designed to encourage these influential individuals to spread word-of-mouth buzz about your brand to their networks. It works because of the power of third-party credibility, and because the endorsement doesn't feel like a sales pitch. It's one clear way to counteract consumers' growing tendency to ignore traditional marketing.

Celebrity endorsements are one way of using influencer marketing tactics, but almost all of the time, that endorsement is transparent, since the Federal Trade Commission now restricts stealth marketing — third-party endorsements that aren't disclosed.

Instead of thinking solely about celebrity endorsements, you might consider focusing on other local influencers. There are three basic kinds of non-celebrity influencers you could partner with: the media elite, like journalists and bloggers; the culturally elite, like socialites or other trendsetters in your market; and the socially connected, like the leaders of your community or business groups, high-powered networkers, and those in your market with a significant social media presence. The key is finding the right influencers to target and properly motivating them to talk about your brand.

Before you select your influencers, consider how many people their message might reach, whether or not they have obvious agendas that could harm your brand, how often they communicate with their networks, and how persuasive they are. Some influencers simply push out other people's content, instead of having strong opinions of their own. You're looking for people who passionately voice their own opinions, not someone who will parrot everything you say, as consumers can appreciate the difference.

Don't confuse popularity with influence. Just because someone is well-known doesn't necessarily mean that they have real influence over the buying decisions of your prospective customers.

Once you've identified your influencer group, which might only be four to six people, then determine what motivation you'll offer them to speak up about your brand. You might ask for feedback on a new product or service, then ask them to share that feedback with their networks. You might invite your influencers to an exclusive event, knowing that the possibility of networking with other influencers might be incentive enough to get them to RSVP. You might also offer them a gift or reward for trying your product and service, as well as one that they could opt to offer to their followers in the form of a contest.

Motivate your influencers to share their positive experiences with your brand, and you could get an entirely new wave of consumers looking your way.

TAKING IT TO THE STREETS

GUERRILLA MARKETING is by definition unconventional. Because it relies more on creativity and sweat equity than on a company's financial investment to give you a big buzz for your buck, it can be a great option for smaller and mid-sized companies that are quick on their feet.

One of the most common forms of guerrilla marketing is the street team. These are groups of volunteers or employees who are working together to promote a product, brand or event through face-to-face interaction with consumers in a public place.

Before you can succeed with street-team marketing, you have to grab the attention of your consumer, even if you're at an event or location where there is significant "noise" competing for your customers' focus. Next, you have to get something into their hands that they won't immediately discard. Finally, you need to leave a lasting, favorable impression. That's a lot to ask of a quick on-the-street consumer interaction, which is why the strongest street teams use innovative strategies for engaging the public that go beyond handing out samples and flyers.

While promoting a new show called "The Event," NBC hired five guys to dress like Secret Service agents and stand outside of Comic-Con, the annual comic fan convention. In a sea of over-the-top costumes, five guys dressed in black suits with dark shades standing motionless, side-by-side, attracted a lot of attention. The "agents" held folders clearly marked "Confidential Information." Instead of approaching consumers, they waited for consumers to come to them.

When people inquired about the folders' contents, the agents responded that it was "highly sensitive" and "dangerous." Some received an official-looking document detailing the escape of a high-profile inmate, with a few words blacked out — but when the visible keywords from the document were entered into Google, it took consumers to a website about the show. Needless to say, the campaign grabbed consumers' attention, put something in their hands, and left a favorable impression that encouraged participants to tell others, so NBC's street team was a solid success.

Once you know how you want to approach your consumers, the keys to making street teams work are recruitment, training, organization, goal setting, measurement and compensation.

Recruit the right members of your team, who are energetic, extroverted brand loyalists. Train them to successfully execute your street-team campaign by showing them how. Assign new members to shadow veteran members until it's time to remove the training wheels.

Organize your teams with team captains who are responsible for coaching in the field and monitoring performance; then set goals for team members and track their performance. For example, team members could have a different code on the coupons they deliver to consumers, so you know which members of your street team are driving the most sales. Follow through by compensating team members based on their performance. You could reward them with a financial payout, but you could also compensate them with something less traditional, like merchandise, a free product, discounts or VIP status at your store.

If you're looking for an inexpensive way to create buzz about your brand and generate traffic, consider taking your message to the streets.

THE CHARMIN EXPERIENCE

LET'S FACE IT: consumers are simply bombarded with marketing clutter everywhere they turn. Standing out from the pack takes ingenuity, which is at the heart of guerrilla marketing.

Experiential marketing, one technique many companies borrow from the guerrilla marketing playbook, allows prospective customers to interact with your brands, products and services in sensory ways. The most successful experiential campaigns utilize as many of the five senses as possible, allowing consumers to see, hear, touch, smell and even taste your product. This full-sensory experience invites consumers to connect emotionally with your brand.

Experiential marketing creates a level of sensory engagement that most print ads or billboards can't. It's about creating dialogue and a buzz of two-way communication, and assuming the experience is positive, experiential marketing can be a fast track to your customers' wallets.

After all, customers want memorable experiences, and they are often willing to pay a premium for them. Disney isn't selling vacations; they're selling memories that last a lifetime. Apple isn't really selling computers; they're selling a lifestyle experience, which is why Apple stores are designed to encourage customers to actively engage with their products.

While Apple products may be an obvious choice for experiential marketing, would you ever think that toilet paper could be?

Charmin rented a two-story space in Times Square and converted it into the "Charmin Restrooms." The Charmin Bear mascots urged passersby to make a pit stop and test-drive their toilet paper, which wasn't a difficult sell considering the shortage of public restrooms in Times Square. Visitors passed under flat screens that broadcasted the Charmin theme song and were escorted to one of 20 luxurious, pristinely clean powder rooms with an abundant supply of Charmin. Visitors could learn the Charmin cha-cha or be entertained by the Charmin bears juggling rolls of toilet paper.

Does this type of marketing work? In a 2006 study conducted by global brand-experience agency, Jack Morton, survey respondents ranked experiential marketing as the number one marketing technique that's most likely to result in a purchase. Eighty percent of respondents indicated experiential marketing leads to a greater understanding of the brand, and 50 percent of respondents indicated they would share their experiences with someone through word of mouth or engage with the company after the experience, online or in person.

Creating opportunities for in-depth consumer interaction with your products goes far beyond just providing samples, and it's particularly useful for brands with complex features and selling points that aren't easily explained within the confines of a traditional advertisement.

You don't have to be a big brand to win at experiential marketing. Consider the kitchen store that offers free cooking classes or the plant nursery that coaches you on creating an herb garden. They're actually creating experiences around your product interaction.

Experiential marketing is the difference between telling people about your brand attributes and allowing them to experience the brand on their own. What multi-sensory experience can you create to drive customer interaction with your product or service?

USE PR AS WEAPON AGAINST COMPETITION

WITH SO MUCH DIGITAL MEDIA and advertising noise cluttering the marketplace, getting noticed by prospective customers has become increasingly difficult. It all boils down to two choices: you can design a wildly creative and compelling campaign, or you can rely on the sheer volume of your messaging. However, creativity and messaging volume both come at a steep cost, so supplementing your advertising with public relations is a good way to stretch a limited advertising budget and generate an overall stronger return on your marketing investment.

PR, or public relations, provides an organization with exposure to prospective consumers, featuring topics of public interest covered by reporters or bloggers. Consumers think this kind of third-party endorsement is more credible than a traditional advertisement. In fact, many experts estimate PR carries three times more credibility than an ad in the eyes of consumers. If managed properly, PR can be a powerful marketing strategy.

PR is most often used as a supplemental strategy to advertising, but it's not a complete replacement. Why? You can control the message, look and feel of your advertisements, helping your consumers gain familiarity with your brand due to that consistent brand and messaging. Plus, a well researched and planned schedule will ensure you reach the right number of targeted consumers with enough frequency to help drive them to make a purchasing decision.

PR comes in many forms but is always less controllable. Someone on your staff might write bylined articles or media commentary, leaders might give media interviews, and even public speaking engagements can count as PR. When developing your PR strategy, it's vital to begin with an assessment of your firm's assets, starting with your CEO.

Does your CEO inspire others with his industry knowledge? If so, your CEO could write a recurring column for a trade magazine, newspaper or even start blogging. Does your CEO shine in front of an audience, captivating them with stories? If so, your CEO might be cut out for public speaking or TV interviews. If your CEO shies away from the limelight, you might propose phone interviews with print reporters at the local newspaper. Play to your strengths.

Once you have a strategy in place, next you'll want to establish relationships with reporters and editors who influence the PR channels you're targeting. However, reporters like to know you've done your homework. You need to know what industries they cover, the types of stories they gravitate toward, and their writing style. They want to see that you are thoughtfully pitching them specifically, not just including them on a mass distribution of a press release.

When you have developed a relationship with a member of the media, make sure the communication goes both ways. Don't always reach out with a need. Support these reporters by making community connections for them when they're trying to land an interview. Send story leads that don't directly benefit your company.

If your media connections see you as a responsive resource, they are more apt to be open to your story ideas.

PR: CATERPILLAR OR BUTTERFLY?

GEORGE CARLIN said it best: "The caterpillar does all the work, but the butterfly gets all the publicity." It's true. Butterflies are just more newsworthy.

Most businesses today can appreciate the important role that PR (public relations) plays in building a brand and creating awareness. Generating press, however, can be more difficult than it sounds, but it all starts with making sure your story is a newsworthy butterfly that has something interesting to say.

It may seem easy, but what's newsworthy to you may fall flat when pitched to a reporter. Just working hard or satisfying your customers isn't newsworthy.

Many factors can influence whether a reporter sees a story worth writing about, but if your story idea meets at least two of these criteria, you'll have a higher chance of success.

In my early days in PR, a reporter asked me a simple question I'll never forget. He asked, "What makes it interesting — right now?"

The story you're pitching needs to be relevant, but it also needs to be timely. Is your company celebrating a milestone anniversary? Do you have a new CEO? Do you offer a product that solves consumer problems that have been in the news this week?

Reporters also consider proximity. How close is your event to the publication's readers or the TV station's viewers, geographically? If you are opening a new location 250 miles away, your local news media may not be interested.

Pitching a story with a novelty factor can also be appealing to news media. When partners in a law firm donate free legal services to those in need, it's not unusual. When those partners roll up their sleeves to rebuild a family's home recently destroyed by a storm, that's unexpected and potentially newsworthy. Make it clear how your story is unexpected.

Reporters also consider your story's significance when they decide whether or not it's newsworthy. How many people does your story impact? If you're pitching a story regarding your company's expansion, it matters whether you are hiring two employees or 200. Even if your company is only hiring two new people, that can still be significant if you connect your new positions to a national trend, like the rising number of successful start-ups that were founded after the flood of corporate layoffs during the recession.

Conflict also breeds interest. If you are a business owner with an opinion about a controversial new retail chain coming to town, that could be newsworthy. If you're in health care and you unite with peers from competing organizations to comment collectively about a controversial component of healthcare reform, that's definitely newsworthy.

Not surprisingly, reporters also like stories with human-interest angles that appeal to the readers' emotions — joy, sadness or even just amusement. TV news programs, for example, often end on a positive note with a feel-good story. These stories bypass the typical criteria for what makes a story news-worthy. They don't need to be timely, novel or significant — but they do need to inspire warm, fuzzy feelings for the audience.

Help your business generate the press it deserves by making sure your stories are newsworthy, so that your brand gets recognized for its good work. Be the butterfly.

AN INSPIRED PITCH

ONE PERCENT. That's how many elevator pitches are unique and inspired. Fortunately, though, it's relatively easy to correct a bad one.

Elevator pitches are concise, planned and practiced descriptions about your company that your mother should be able to understand in the time it would take to ride an elevator — about 60 seconds.

It's a vital tool for creating awareness and gaining the interest of a prospect. It can be used in networking settings, at social events, during meetings with new prospects, or when anyone says, "What do you do?" Since so few compelling pitches are being delivered, having a strong elevator pitch is a fairly simple, no-cost way to stand miles apart from your competitors.

Dynamic, inspired elevator pitches deliver the big message that sets your company apart, but it should also capture someone's imagination. It should be filled with impact, personality and intensity. Most importantly, it should leave the listener asking to learn more.

Strong, dynamic elevator pitches have four key ingredients.

#1: Your elevator pitch should include a brief description of what you do, without using any jargon. Mine starts out very simply — "I'm a sales coach and marketer." Titles aren't important. Your objective isn't to impress prospects with your credentials, but to leave your prospect with a clear understanding of what you do in language they might actually understand and remember. Don't just explain what you do for the company; make it personal.

#2: Your elevator pitch should also describe specifically what you do for your clients in distinct language. Make sure you avoid vague, overused, and self-congratulatory statements, like when someone says, "We solve our client's problems," or "We form a partnership with our customers." Instead of using tired clichés, consider offering specific reasons why your clients like your company. Start with something straight-forward, like "Our clients hire us because...."

#3: Next, you should provide a real example of how your company helped a customer overcome a challenge, explaining your points of differentiation in the process. You want to share a vibrant story of how you helped one, particular customer; so don't list everything you could ever possibly do to help a client. However, it's very important that the story you choose conveys what makes your company different from competitors.

#4: Finally, you should illustrate the impact you had for the client you just mentioned. It helps if the results that you generated for that client are tangible — like a specific amount of cost savings, the exact amount of revenue you generated, or the percentage efficiency you helped the client gain.

Once you've developed your elevator pitch, rehearse it. Once you've finished rehearsing, rehearse again, and then rehearse some more. Don't wing it. You want your pitch to sound conversational, but it needs to be polished. Remember that you have one shot of capturing your prospects' imaginations, and piquing their interest in what you do. Make every single word count.

Even the most well-crafted elevator pitch will fall flat without a strong, engaging delivery. Deliver yours with inflection and enthusiasm, being sure to connect with your audience by varying the volume and pace of key phrases in your pitch for emphasis. Pitch with presence and conviction.

Believe in your pitch, or else no one else will. Pitch like your livelihood depends on it, because it does.

SALES: MISSING INGREDIENT IN PR

IF YOUR COMPANY'S CONTRIBUTIONS are newsworthy, but you still aren't getting much media coverage, you could have a sales problem. That's right, I said a "sales" problem.

The minimum cost of entry into a career in public relations, or PR, is the ability to write. Most people in PR have strong writing skills, and they're perfectly capable of inspiring readers with the written word. However, because of the sheer volume of press releases crossing the average reporter's desk each week, writing skills alone won't land stories.

Above-average PR professionals also have strong relationship-building skills with reporters and editors, allowing them to garner more media attention than their writing-focused counterparts.

Stellar PR pros couple their writing and relationship-building skills with the finesse of a veteran sales consultant. Very few in the profession wield these unique powers of persuasion, which is why having these skills allows you and your company to stand apart from your colleagues and competitors in a remarkable way.

Supporting this premise, PR Newswire reports that just 55 percent of its stories get picked up — no doubt a result of less than stellar pitching or sales skills. To generate a different result, you must transform your approach.

Much like the steps in a sales pitch, begin your PR pitch by establishing a relationship with a reporter, which begins by doing your homework. Read a variety of the reporter's work. Know his or her beat, style and common story angles. Use social media to learn about a reporter's interests. Use this information to engage and connect with each reporter you call.

Then offer the reporter an inspired 30-second elevator pitch about your company — just enough to pique his interest — followed by a request to ask a few questions. Your questions and the reporter's answers will allow you to tailor the story angle you're proposing based on the outlet's content needs. Explain your desire to make the best use of both of your time.

Proceed with your needs assessment by asking open-ended questions to get the reporter engaged in the conversation and to identify content needs with which you may be able to assist. There is a direct correlation between the time a reporter spends talking and your likelihood to land a story.

Next, restate the content needs and story opportunities that you learned from the reporter. If applicable, offer up a content suggestion by explaining what makes it newsworthy today, how it's unique, and why the reporter's readers will care.

At this point, you've earned the right to ask for the story outright. If you get anything other than a definitive yes, go back to the needs assessment. Inquire further about what's causing the reporter's pause, uncovering any objections, resolving them and attempting to close again.

By taking a relationship-based sales approach to public relations, you have the ability to dominate local media in your category.

TOP TEN PR PITFALLS

WHILE THERE'S NO one-size-fits-all checklist that will ensure you never make a PR misstep, there are some common pitfalls you should avoid to give yourself the best possible chance for in-depth, meaningful media coverage.

Don't bury the lead. The more content a reporter must sift through to get to the main point of your pitch, the more likely it is that your pitch goes into the trash. Get to the point, and get there fast.

If you aren't enthusiastic about what you are pitching, you can't expect others to be enthusiastic either. Smile when you pitch. Turn up the energy. By all means, talk to the reporter instead of reading from a script.

Don't send your press release to multiple reporters in the same office. It just calls attention to the fact that you haven't done your homework, and it makes it seem like you aren't sure who to pitch. It can also cause confusion in the newsroom. It's even worse if you "CC" every reporter in town. At the very least, "BCC" those on your distribution list, though it's best to select targeted reporters, writing each one a personal note.

Don't pitch the wrong reporter. Reporters cover different topics, and the beats they cover frequently change. Make sure you double check that the reporter you're contacting still covers your industry before you send your pitch.

If you are pitching the story on Twitter, make sure you follow the reporter so he can reply with a private direct message that the general public can't see.

Try to avoid leaving voicemail messages for reporters, but if you must, make sure you provide enough important facts to whet their appetites. Unless your relationship with a reporter is rock-solid, teaser voicemails that are intentionally vague don't typically get reporters to dial your number.

Don't lose credibility by acting like there's life-changing news when there's not. Resist the temptation to overhype.

Buzzwords don't impress busy reporters and editors. Get to the point, using straightforward language that is easy to understand.

Don't ignore your competitors' PR efforts. If the reporter you're pitching has already written a story on a competitor, ensure that your story has a different angle.

Don't limit yourself to local PR. Consider distributing your release to a broader distribution of reporters regionally or even nationally. Services like PRNewswire or PRWeb can help you cast a wide net to get a broader audience.

Properly managed, your public relations strategy can be a powerful, sophisticated marketing tool, but make sure you're following these tips to get the results you want.

PR CRISIS: THE INTERSECTION OF DANGER AND OPPORTUNITY

WE'VE ALL HEARD the myth that "all PR is good PR." We also know that this isn't always the case.

Many business owners think that a PR crisis can only happen to large companies, like BP after the Deepwater Horizon oil spill, or government entities, like FEMA when it was cleaning up the aftermath of Hurricane Katrina. However, smaller companies rely on a smaller customer base. Losing one or two large customers due to a mismanaged PR crisis could cripple the bottom line for any small or mid-sized business. If you can see a potential crisis coming and plan accordingly, though, your PR response can mitigate risk to your brand's reputation, improve customer loyalty and even generate new customers.

Because you never know when a crisis might occur, it is always good to have a crisis-management plan in place. Consider these tips to get you started.

Identify your vulnerabilities: What scenarios put you at risk for negative PR? Robberies? Stolen or lost system data? Safety-related injuries? Employees behaving unethically? Disgruntled customers talking to the media? By identifying your vulnerabilities in advance, you can have a plan in place so that you're prepared for the worst-case scenario.

Identify your key audiences: Which groups will you need to communicate with about any of these crises? Customers and prospects? Vendors? Employees and strategic partners? Keep your list of these contacts current, and make that list easily accessible for crisis team members.

Establish processes for gathering information: While it's important to act quickly in crisis mode, it's also vital that you have accurate information, so that you can speak knowledgably and avoid missteps. Establish communication protocols for conveying critical information.

Appoint a crisis spokesperson: For a small business, it's best to appoint one spokesperson, and provide that person with media training. As we learned from BP during the Deepwater Horizon oil spill, the right person isn't always the CEO. BP's CEO, Tony Hayward, will always be remembered for callously stating, "There's no one who wants this over more than I do. I would like my life back." Choose someone who can communicate clearly and diplomatically.

Choose a business attorney: During a crisis, consulting an attorney is helpful. Interview attorneys in advance to find one you trust with experience consulting on crises for similar companies in your industry.

Create a process for addressing complaints: Create a year-round process for tracking all complaints, and establish a timeline for response.

If you should have the misfortune of dealing with a PR crisis, act quickly to resolve the situation and always tell the truth. Don't evade critics; face them. Provide regular updates to all of your key stakeholders, while demonstrating both confidence and compassion.

You will also need to be accessible to media, early and often. Avoiding the media only means that you won't have the opportunity to tell your side of the story.

Finally, don't hesitate to apologize and correct a situation when necessary. Take responsibility. John F. Kennedy, a seasoned PR pro, often reminded his staff that the word "crisis" written in Chinese is composed of two characters: one that represents danger and another that represents opportunity. Be prepared for both.

SOUTHWEST SHOWS RIGHT MODEL FOR SURVIVING CRISES

MOST OF OUR ATTENTION typically goes to big brands making bigger blunders in the face of a crisis, so it's refreshing to celebrate a brand getting it right.

Southwest Airlines regularly deploys a combination of strategies to ensure that it not only survives inevitable PR crises, but emerges as a stronger brand afterward. Because of Southwest's exemplary crisis management, it is throwing down a gauntlet that challenges all brands — large or small — to examine their own readiness for a crisis and to develop or strengthen their plans accordingly.

Southwest Crisis No. 1 — Facebook Frenzy: When Southwest was celebrating its three-millionth Facebook fan, it offered significant airfare deals exclusively through Facebook. The promotion was much more popular than expected. Soon, the Southwest system was overwhelmed by a flood of reservations, resulting in customers who were billed more than once for the same airfare.

Southwest very quickly and publicly owned up to the mistake by explaining how it would be corrected and avoided in the future.

While some customers were understandably unhappy, many others jumped to praise Southwest's speedy response because of all the goodwill the brand had built through years of doing right by its customers.

Southwest Crisis No. 2 — Emergency Tweet: Thanks to the instantaneous nature of social media and the availability of in-air Wi-Fi, the world can hear about an in-air emergency before the pilot even has a chance to report it. This was the case when a hole tore open in the body of a Southwest plane flying from Phoenix, AZ to Sacramento, CA. The brand's social media managers, who monitor the Internet relentlessly, quickly spotted the tweet and posted a rapid response on the brand's blog.

Southwest Crisis No. 3 — Nose Gear Failure: When the landing gear under the nose of a Southwest plane landing at LaGuardia collapsed, the plane had to make an emergency landing, and there were several injured passengers. Southwest's rapid response team was online addressing the incident 30 minutes after the flight landed, which is significantly faster than the industry norm.

As you can see, the Southwest communications team is masterful at getting out in front of a story and controlling its direction through open, honest communication. Comments from Southwest spokesman, Paul Flannigan, show that the communications team is actually busier when nothing is going on, constantly updating contingency plans and pre-approved statements in preparation for possible crises. Everyone on the Southwest communications team is clear about how to make rapid responses possible.

Couple Southwest's crisis planning with its year-round positive reputation, and you have a solid crisis-management formula that will allow Southwest to survive just about any PR turbulence.

SPOKESPERSON OFFERS BRANDS LARGER VOICE

PARTNERING WITH a brand spokesperson can give your message a larger voice while also transferring the positive feelings the market has for that spokesperson over to your brand. But how do you know if a spokesperson makes sense for your brand?

Begin by asking these five questions. Is your target market fairly broad? Does public perception play a large role in driving customers to your brand? Do you aspire for a notable shift in that public perception? Do you have something transformational to communicate to the marketplace? Is your brand's circle of influence smaller than ideal?

If you answered "yes" to many of these questions, you may want to consider a spokesperson partnership. In selecting a spokesperson for your company, consider these guidelines.

Think about whether your target market will respond most positively to a local celebrity, someone with social influence, or a business authority speaking on behalf of your brand.

Make sure the spokesperson's lifestyle and symbolic identity in the market-place are both aligned with your brand. The personal traits of the spokesperson must be compatible with the traits of your brand.

Assess the spokesperson's credibility or trustworthiness. Research press coverage and social-media activity related to your prospective spokesperson for the last several years. Get feedback from your customers about the spokesperson. What words come to their minds when they think of that person?

Finally, it is crucial to partner with a spokesperson who believes in your brand and vision.

Perhaps the most perfectly aligned brand spokesperson of all time was Michael Jordan for Nike. With a long-time campaign slogan of "Just Do It," Nike generally doesn't focus on its products in its advertising campaigns. Instead, Nike honors great athletes and their abilities — stretching the limits of what can be, athletically. Who better to reinforce that message than Jordan, perhaps the greatest basketball player of all time and certainly a credible spokesperson regarding all things athletics? What's more, Jordan has a high trust factor in the marketplace. He had enough impact on Nike for the shoe brand to design a line of sneakers after him.

In the mid-1970s, formerly strong sales of JELL-O, including its pudding line, began declining, and so the brand hired 37-year-old comedian and actor Bill Cosby to serve as spokesperson. It was a perfect alignment for both the JELL-O and Cosby brands at the time, as each shared a wholesome, family-oriented image, which would later be called into question in Cosby's case. The partnership was so beneficial for the snack brand that it maintained a relationship with the actor for nearly three decades, ending in 2003 — well before a personal scandal dominated Cosby's brand image. It's considered the longest celebrity endorsement in American advertising history.

A spokesperson can be beneficial for small and large companies alike. Just do your homework to ensure proper "fit," be aware of the risks, and make sure that the anticipated benefits justify that risk and expense.

DRIVE SALES WITH A CAUSE

RALLYING FOR A CAUSE you feel passionate about feels good, but it can also make good business sense. According to a 2013 study by Cone Cause Evolution, 89 percent of consumers would consider switching brands if they found a new brand that aligned itself with a good cause.

41 percent of Americans said they have purchased a product in the past year because of a cause, which is twice the percentage that agreed with that statement when Cone first introduced the question in 1993.

Cause marketing is a marketing alliance that pairs a company with a social cause so that they can both mutually benefit. If you want to leverage your social capital, consider these types of cause-marketing campaigns.

Transactional cause-marketing campaigns trigger a donation when your customer makes a purchase. Yoplait's "Friends in the Fight" campaign donates 10 cents to one of three breast-cancer charities, selected by consumers, for every pink Yoplait lid consumers register online.

With event campaigns, your company partners with a charity to host a fundraising event such as a 5K, a walk-a-thon or a food festival.

Digital campaigns rely on websites, email and social media to spread the word about your cause, encouraging consumers to take action online by donating, volunteering, purchasing merchandise, liking a page or by making a message go viral.

With sweat-equity campaigns, employees roll up their sleeves to physically help out a local charity by building a Habitat for Humanity house, for example. If you select a cause that aligns with your brand, a sweat-equity campaign has a good chance of creating a strong association for consumers between your brand and the good work you're doing in the community. These types of campaigns lend themselves well to generating media attention because of the compelling imagery. If that isn't enough reason to sway you toward a sweat-equity campaign, many people believe it is no longer enough for corporations to just make financial contributions to charities. They want to see companies getting involved and integrating good causes into their day-to-day business.

Companies looking to develop a cause-marketing strategy should also give careful consideration to selecting the right cause. The cause you choose needs to align with your brand, but it should also be a cause that your employees are passionate about. Huggies created its own charity, the "Every Little Bottom" program, which provides diapers for needy children. Macy's supports the Make-a-Wish Foundation through its "Believe" holiday campaign. Kids drop letters to Santa into Macy's store letterboxes or email them online, and the retailer donates $1 to Make-a-Wish for every letter.

Once you've selected your cause, work with the charity's organizers to set donation targets and to define how the campaign will increase your visibility. It can help expand your reach and increase awareness of your brand if the charity will promote your campaign through its own website, emails, newsletters, social-media channels and direct-mail efforts.

Finally, launch a well-planned, multi-channel marketing effort promoting your cause-marketing campaign. People will need to see your message frequently if your campaign is going to motivate them to switch companies. One press release won't do it, so use a variety of messaging platforms to reach prospective customers in multiple ways to raise awareness of your company's cause and your selected charity as well.

ART AND SCIENCE OF ADVERTISING

ADVERTISING OPPORTUNITIES are so plentiful that it can be hard to know which method is most likely to generate a strong return. Without a comprehensive advertising plan, you may find yourself making impulsive one-time ad purchases, which are unlikely to produce results.

How do you evaluate the various advertising opportunities that come your way? Begin by defining your target audience. If you define your target market as 35- to 45-year-old male homeowners in a particular ZIP code with household incomes of $100K-plus, you're not precluding others from doing business with you. You're focusing your ad investment on the segment that provides the greatest opportunity. The more narrowly defined the target audience, the more often you can afford to get your message in front of that group, which will increase the chance of your target audience doing business with your company.

Next, determine how to reach your target-audience members by determining which communication channels they use the most. How? Try asking them. Survey existing customers that fit the profile of your target audience. It's not enough to just know Generation Y is most tapped into digital ad channels. In your market, what specific websites and social media tools do they use the most?

Compare these findings to audience demographics provided by each media outlet of interest to determine the ideal mix. Be sure to consider how the surrounding editorial content and mix of advertisers align with your brand image.

Crafting an advertising schedule is both an art and a science. Begin by assessing the value of the expense by calculating the CPM (cost per thousand, with the "M" representing the roman numeral for 1000) — a tool to compare advertising expense across channels (e.g., TV compared to print). It's not an exact science, as it assumes a TV viewer is equivalent to a print viewer, which isn't the case given how frequently TV viewers skip commercials. Regardless, it does provide you with at least a starting point for comparison.

To calculate CPM, divide the total number of impressions (people projected to see the ad as reported by a third-party research firm for the newspaper, magazine or TV station) by 1000. Then divide the total cost of the ad by that number. So let's say a print ad costs $1500 and will generate a reported 10,000 impressions. Begin your calculation by taking 10,000 divided by 1000, which equals 10. Then divide $1500 by 10 to get a CPM of $150.

Once an advertising channel has been selected, determine the appropriate frequency needed to motivate your target audience to take the desired action. There's an old adage that consumers must see an advertisement seven times before making a decision to buy. In reality, the right frequency depends on subjective factors. If consumers are already familiar with your brand, you won't need as much frequency to drive consumer action. If customers are unlikely to have awareness of your brand, you will need more frequency to get their attention. Remember, too, that emotional messages tend to drive consumers to take action more quickly, even without as much frequency.

Once you've selected an advertising strategy, stick with it long enough to really test it out. If you're considering putting all of your ad dollars into a single ad placement and can't afford any others, use your money elsewhere. Without frequency, you're unlikely to gain traction in the market.

HOW TO ADAPT TO TODAY'S VISUAL CULTURE

GREAT ADVERTISING engages our senses. While we may not be able to touch or taste a product through an ad, with the right image, we get a sense for what it's like by looking through someone else's eyes.

Compelling imagery draws us in and helps us experience the brand, if only virtually. In fact, Victoria University researchers discovered in 2013 that consumers are more likely to trust a brand when images are present in its advertising.

In 2012, a synopsis of research from sources like The New York Times, National Retail Federation and PR Newswire was compiled by MDG Agency with surprising results. Articles with images get 94 percent more views than those without. Including a photo in a press release increases the number of views by 45 percent. Over 60 percent of consumers are more likely to contact a business when an image shows up in local search-engine results. On e-commerce sites, 67 percent of consumers say the quality of the image is "very important" in selecting a product for purchase — even more important than product information and consumer ratings.

Why has there been this significant shift toward images? According to Photofocus, in 2013, there were an estimated 5.2 billion cellphone cameras used, and 90 percent of people have taken pictures with a camera phone.

This has led to two interesting trends: 1) There's been a significant increase in photo creation, with Time Magazine reporting in 2012 that 10 percent of all photos ever taken in the history of mankind occurred over the last year, and 2) Photos are becoming the new universal language for younger generations, especially in light of social-media phenoms Pinterest and Instagram.

Because of the popularity of personal photography, consumers have also grown tired of traditional, carefully styled photographs; so smart marketers are now using photos consumers might have actually taken and shared on social networks themselves. In fact, upscale retail brands like Tiffany and Coach have dedicated street-style photographers that create digital ad campaigns to share on Facebook, Pinterest and other websites. Even though Lancôme is a traditional brand, it took a risk and hired a makeup artist with a large YouTube following to create homemade "how to" videos with its products, and those videos saw a million views in just a few short days.

If you're advertising a brand, it is important to realize that imagery is more important now than ever before, and consumers' preferences are shifting. The presence of authentic, less manufactured imagery engages buyers — and that engagement can drive sales.

NARROWCASTING KILLS BROADCAST ADVERTISING

IF YOU'RE STILL OPERATING under the advertising principles that worked 10 years ago, your brand equity and customer base may be slipping away before your eyes. In many ways, the strategies that work today are the polar opposites of tactics that worked even just a decade ago.

Under the old rules, we created products and services that appealed to the masses and advertised them in that way, broadcasting to as large an audience as possible with a generic message that appealed to most people. We earned growth by building mass-market awareness around our brands, and then leveraging that consumer familiarity by creating product-line extensions with the same kind of mass appeal.

Those days are gone.

In today's reality, the sheer volume of media outlets, along with the Internet, has created a highly fragmented marketplace. Brands can easily identify smaller groups of buyers and focus on those distinct interests and communication preferences. Thanks to small-batch manufacturing, new distribution options and the infinitely more detailed consumer data available to marketers, consumers have come to expect brands to communicate with them in a highly personalized way. You could refuse to adapt to this environment, but consumers are simply tuning out messaging that doesn't speak to them directly. It's easy for them to ignore you, after all, especially with the tremendous amount of promotional content they are exposed to every day.

The strategy to thrive in this new reality is called narrowcasting, which involves targeting media messages at specific segments defined by shared values, demographic attributes or preferences.

What are the new rules of narrowcasting?

Rule No. 1: Narrow your target market to a specific niche, instead of trying to be all things to all people. The narrower your focus becomes, the better, provided you don't limit your pool of buyers so much that you forfeit growth.

Rule No. 2: Regularly ask consumers within your niche what they want and expect from your brand, then develop products and services accordingly. Great brands listen to the marketplace and respond quickly. They don't just decide on their own what's most important to consumers. This is a more egalitarian approach to research and development.

Rule No. 3: Make sure your messaging and the marketing channels you use to promote that messaging are both a perfect fit for your brand's specific niche. The days of casting a wide advertising net are over.

Brands that will excel in this new narrowcasting environment may not appeal to the masses, but they will establish brand loyalty among narrow niches of consumers by creating a highly customized experience that is tailored and relevant. They will position themselves as specialists that can anticipate and nimbly adapt to the needs of their target audience, and they will ultimately be rewarded with greater profitability than ever before.

PSYCHOLOGY BEHIND PERSUASIVE HEADLINES

IF YOU ARE WRITING lackluster headlines, you are wasting your time. Your marketing content will never be read.

Too often, headlines seem to be an afterthought, which is a colossal misstep. Copyblogger reported in 2015 that 8 out of the 10 people who see your headline will read it, but only 2 out of those 8 people will read the accompanying article — and that's only if your headline is compelling.

Research conducted in 2011 by KISSmetrics indicates the perfect length for a headline is six words or less, since people have a tendency to scan the first and last three words of a longer headline.

How can you write a truly persuasive headline? Try these six proven strategies for writing compelling headlines that will leave your readers wanting more.

Shock: Readers love novelty. Surprising headlines activate the pleasure centers in our brains much more than seeing content we already know about, because we prefer the unpredictable to the known subconsciously. For example, one headline that might grab your attention might read, "Surprising facts about your home security risks."

Curiosity: Sparking a reader's interest by asking a question can be a persuasive headline strategy, assuming you know the right question to ask. Simply seeing a question mark springs your brain into action as you think about your answer. If your headline is a question, make sure you feel confident your audience will want to see it answered.

Problem solving: Our brains are hardwired to solve problems. When a writer presents a headline that seems to speak to the unique problems we face, we tune in. For example, one headline that will speak to many readers might say, "For people who are prone to running injuries, but love to run."

Negativity: Perhaps because negative headlines are unexpected — or possibly because they trigger the reader's insecurities — negative headlines generally outperform their positive counterparts significantly, whether we like it or not. After all, we've all responded to negative headlines that say things like "Avoid these five foods to improve energy."

Lists: Most people like it when articles are neatly packaged into numbered lists. In fact, a 2014 CoSchedule study analyzed more than one million blog post headlines and reported numbered lists outperformed any other headline by nearly double.

How-To: Every day, we all have entirely too many tasks to accomplish, too many priorities to sort, too much information to digest, and not enough time for any of it. If your headline tells your readers how to gain control of their lives and make better sense of things, you're likely to have a lively readership.

Headlines matter more than you would think. If you are going to write content, plan to spend at least half of your writing time developing an attention-grabbing, persuasive headline. It's an investment that can pay big dividends.

ONLINE ADVERTISING STRATEGIES

U.S. SPENDING in online advertising was projected to rise 16 percent in 2015 compared to the prior year, according to eMarketer. While the percentage increase may be surprising, no one is shocked by the increasing shift from offline to online channels.

Despite the explosion of digital advertising over the last decade, many small and mid-sized companies have yet to wade into these waters too deeply, as the landscape is complex and the perceived cost of entry high. While there is much to know about the nuances of online advertising, it begins with an understanding of these three common options: display ads, native ads and search ads.

Display ads are essentially banner ads that redirect a user to a website. They are generally purchased on a CPM (cost per 1000 impressions) or CPC (cost per click) basis.

Display ads offer a relatively low cost-per-click, considering the high number of people exposed to the ad. They also allow for visually appealing ads with graphics that support branding. However, display ads typically generate a low click-through rate, due in part to the limited control you have over who sees or clicks your ad, with the potential for many of those clicks to be accidental.

Even if the people clicking your ad are not truly interested in your brand, you still pay for their clicks if you've agreed to a cost-per-click payment arrangement.

Native ads are similar to display ads in the way they are purchased, but they allow the ad to appear directly in user newsfeeds, on Facebook and Twitter for example, not just in a special advertising section of the site. Display ads are designed to interrupt the users' online activities, while native ads are designed to fit within those activities.

Native ads often generate higher levels of engagement when the content is interesting, relevant to the user and appropriate for the mission of the targeted site. Content that feels overly promotional or otherwise inappropriate for placement within a user's newsfeed will largely be ignored.

Search ads, like those you'd find at the top or right of a Google search, offer highly qualified clicks and high click-through rates, since you're targeting consumers looking for precisely what you're offering, provided you purchase the right keywords, of course. However, you'll often face stiff competition for desirable keywords, which drives up the cost per click — and with just two lines of descriptive text available for brand messaging, your marketing message is very limited.

Don't feel like you have to invest thousands right out of the gate. A few hundred dollars can provide you with an ample test to see if the strategy is right for your brand.

Display ads, native ads and search ads are three easy ways to get started with online marketing, but make sure that you carefully weigh the benefits and drawbacks of each tactic before you invest, so that you can generate the strongest return on your investment.

MOBILE DEPENDENCY ENERGIZES TEXT ADVERTISING

THE AVERAGE CONSUMER generally has at least one mobile device within arm's reach at any given time throughout the day. Our growing dependency on these devices has increased the opportunity for marketers to reach targeted consumers with greater immediacy than ever before via text-message marketing.

When you consider that text message marketing generally carries a 95 percent open rate with 90 percent of texts read within five minutes of receipt, it's no wonder why 38 percent of businesses reported leveraging text-message marketing, according to a 2013 StrongMail study.

If you think that your target market isn't young enough for text marketing, you should think again. Consumers ages 45-54 send and receive an average of 33 texts per day, with those 55 and older averaging 16 texts per day, according to Experian's 2013 Digital Marketer Report. Additionally, Baby Boomers are the largest growing demographic of mobile users.

While text marketing isn't for every business category, it can be extraordinarily effective for business-to-consumer (B2C) brands, like restaurants or bars, hotels and other retail establishments, among others.

If you want to try out a text-message-marketing campaign, make sure you are only messaging people who have knowingly opted in, offer an easy opt-out feature, avoid sending promotional texts outside of business hours, and don't send more than one text per week. Most importantly, be sure to deliver timely, valuable and exclusive content to your mobile subscribers as an incentive for them to remain on your list.

Some of the most effective text-marketing opt-in campaigns are the most straightforward, like asking consumers to text a special keyword to have their names appear on a digital sign at a special event, like the big game or a nightclub, or even for participation in a group poll. You might also consider using this strategy as a way to allow consumers to gain an extra entry into a Facebook drawing.

If you own a grocery store, consider a text-marketing campaign that encourages shoppers to subscribe to your text list for recipes or a same-day coupon. If you run a veterinary office, doctor's office or dental office, leverage text marketing for reminders about annual shots, exams or check-ups that are overdue. Restaurateurs can offer mobile-exclusive specials to drive last-minute reservations on nights that are slow. For those in retail, consider offering early-bird access to special sales in your store for mobile subscribers.

If you are considering testing the text message-marketing waters, make sure to partner with a professional firm that can ensure your execution doesn't expose you to regulatory risks, or worse, the alienation of your customers.

AD RETARGETING MAY SPOIL GIFT-GIVING SURPRISE

WHEN YOU SHOP AMAZON for a product and then see that same product in a Facebook ad days later, that's not a coincidence. It is a marketing strategy called ad retargeting, and it's absolutely dominating online advertising.

Here's how it works: Most consumer-focused websites have long used "cookies" to track your interactions with their sites. The first time you search for a product, the brand's website saves a cookie to your browser that can be read or modified by the site. The site then buys ad space on other consumer websites. When you visit one of those sites, you will see an ad that's been customized for you based on what the cookie already knows.

It's certainly not an exact science. Occasionally, you'll see ads for products you have already bought. However, it often works. CMO.com reported in 2013 that ad retargeting boosts digital-ad responses by 400 percent. While the whole idea may remind you of *Minority Report*, the study indicates that only 11 percent of the market is uncomfortable with retargeted ads. The idea is to deliver more meaningful advertising to consumers, going far beyond a one-size-fits-all mass advertising approach.

The key to retargeting is to deploy it responsibly by delivering ads that consumers are generally comfortable with, avoiding sensitive topics. For example, even if you can tell from digital tracking that a group of consumers might be going through a divorce, advertising books on how to cope with divorce to those consumers isn't a good idea.

Retargeting can work in both the nonprofit and the for-profit world. It is a natural fit for business-to-consumer (B2C) industries, and it can also work in some business-to-business (B2B) categories as well.

As a consumer, you may want to give some thought to how you search for gifts for your significant other. If you share a computer or the same user profile, your loved one could be tipped off about your purchase intentions when that Apple Watch you have been researching begins popping up as a retargeted ad across multiple websites.

Protecting your big surprise is fairly easy, though. In most browsers, simply select "Tell Sites I Do Not Want to Be Tracked" or "Do Not Track" from the Settings menu then select "Privacy" or "Private Browsing" from your browser's drop-down menu. This will prevent tracking until you decide to turn it back on.

If the whole idea of retargeting makes you antsy, keep in mind that these brands aren't likely sharing this data and colluding to sell you. That kind of information exchange just isn't necessary in ad retargeting.

HEY THERE!
WHAT'S YOUR SIGN?

ADVERTISING ICON Steuart Henderson Britt once said, "Doing business without advertising is like winking at a girl in the dark. You know what you are doing, but nobody else does."

It seems obvious, but so many business owners believe that if they build their businesses, customers will come without any advertising at all. However, unless you have a brilliantly unique product or service that creates a significant word-of-mouth buzz on its own, this is not a strong growth strategy.

Billboards may seem dated, but they can still be effective tools for quickly building brand awareness, especially on a trial basis, if you have a fairly broad target audience or one that is distinguished primarily by its geography.

One of the most successful of the early adopters of billboard advertising was Burma Shaving Cream. From the 1920s to 1960s, Burma ran a series of billboards, typically featuring six consecutive small signs posted along the edge of highways, spaced out for sequential reading. Even though multi-sign messaging is no longer as economically feasible, having a billboard is still a strong way to communicate with prospective customers.

Modern-day billboard options include digital billboards, which allow you to change your message more easily and inexpensively, and mobile billboards, which can target a specific neighborhood.

Even though traditional billboards may seem old school, you can always put a new twist on an old idea with guerrilla signage. For example, McDonald's converted an everyday streetlight into what looks like a piping hot stream of coffee by painting the post brown and placing a ridiculously large McDonald's coffee cup beneath it.

To promote a season of its series The Sopranos, HBO hung what looked like the arm of a whacked mob boss — adorned with mob ring, cuff links and the arm of a shiny suit — from the trunk of New York City cabs, along with a Sopranos bumper sticker.

You don't have to be a big brand to have the budget for guerrilla signage. Consider writing clever messages with sidewalk chalk to attract pedestrians, or using street teams to hold signs in front of your store. Consider what's already available that can become part of your billboard. One cigar shop brought wooden telephone poles to life by wrapping large paper cigar bands around them, transforming them into cigars.

Advertising through guerrilla signage isn't just for traditional businesses; nonprofits and municipalities are in the game, too. Denver Water launched a simple, brilliant billboard campaign using only one-third of a billboard, leaving a completely bare billboard frame across the other two-thirds. The conservation-based message reads, "Use only what you need," demonstrating its point by using fewer materials in construction.

When you're planning your next strategy, look around with fresh eyes. Maybe you will see a sign that shows you how guerrilla signage can bring your message to life.

3

The consultative sales model was conceived in the 1970s and was ahead of its time. Its discovery or question-based approach puts the sales person in the enviable role of adviser, and its principles couldn't be more relevant today. At its core is the premise that you must first seek to understand before you can truly be understood. Master this sales methodology, and you will find yourself forging impenetrable, long-term relationships and consistently outpacing competing sales professionals.

EXECUTE YOUR SALES STRATEGY

THE EVOLUTION OF CONSULTATIVE SALES

CONSULTATIVE SALES is a discovery-based approach that puts the sales professional in the enviable role of partner or adviser versus the stereotypical pushy rep looking to close a deal at any cost.

The selling philosophy was born in the 1970s and was ahead of its time. In fact, its principles couldn't be more relevant today, explaining its growing acceptance as the preferred sales methodology over the last couple of decades.

At its core, consultative sales is based on the premise that you must first seek to understand before you can truly be understood. This knowledge of the prospect begins with thorough research conducted prior to the first sales meeting and continues through the lifecycle of that customer relationship through the use of high-impact questions.

The official steps begin with the ever-critical need to establish a relationship with your prospect. The conversation then moves into a needs assessment where a series of research-based customized questions are asked, allowing the sales rep to learn about the prospect's pain and challenges. Armed with that understanding, the consultative sales professional formulates and shares solutions that address the prospect's needs before closing the sale.

Sometimes that sales person's products and services are the solution, but that's often not the case. At the heart of consultative sales is the belief that you have a unique privilege to serve your prospect's needs, whatever those may be. If the better solution for a particular prospect's situation is your lower-priced competitor, then that's what you should recommend. That candor and selflessness can create lifelong advocates for the sales professional and brand.

While these basic tenets are still spot-on today, like any strategy, the consultative sales model must evolve to keep pace. Here are two ways this nearly 50-year-old strategy is evolving.

First, the Information Age has allowed prospective buyers to gain a better understanding of the problems they face and the possible solutions before ever speaking with a sales rep. As such, buyers don't rely as heavily on salespeople to diagnose their problems and map out a course of action. Sure, some buyers with complex problems seek just that, but many simply seek to be understood.

In fact, in the 2015 "What Sales Winners Do Differently" study by the Rain Group, this development became clear. Of the 42 characteristics of a sales rep that drive prospects to buy, "deepened my understanding of my needs" ranked a surprisingly low 40th in importance. In contrast, "understood my needs" was fifth.

Secondly, today's most skilled in sales don't stop with identifying prospect pain. They are also having rich conversations about the prospect's aspirations and dreams, helping prospects visualize what's possible in a partnership. After all, a lack of pain doesn't equate to a lack of potential. Modern consultative sales reps effectively paint a picture of what could be.

TIPS FOR OVERCOMING FEAR OF SELLING

THE WORLD is made up of two kinds of people: those who try, and if they stumble, they dust themselves off and try again; and those who fear stumbling so much that they essentially quit trying. We all know which of the two is more successful in business.

President Franklin Roosevelt said it best, "The only thing we have to fear is fear itself." Fear can paralyze sales teams, keeping them from taking action. It can make them hostages of their own negative thinking, making them avoid trying new approaches or taking risks of any kind.

It can be tough for individuals on your sales teams to admit being afraid, since fear is often equated with weakness. In reality, it's perfectly natural and even healthy to have fears. Fear can lead us to work harder, improving professionally. Not admitting and addressing those fears, though, can be any salesperson's single biggest impediment to success.

There are common excuses salespeople give for not meeting their prospecting activity targets. "I don't want to seem too pushy," or "I'm too busy." "I'm not sure what to say when I call," or even, "They know I'm here, and they'll call when they're ready to buy." Excuses like these are actually rooted in fear.

However, these fears are common. Almost all sales professionals have faced down fears like these during their careers.

When facing these kinds of fears, there are several strategies you can use to overcome your anxieties and ultimately find success:

First, you have to know what scares you. Are you afraid of rejection? Do you fear being offensive or intrusive? Are you worried your clients won't like you? Do you fear not having all the answers? Are you afraid of looking foolish? Most people have the most common anxiety of all: the fear of failure.

Once you've realized what scares you, imagine the worst-case scenario. If your fear is rejection, what is the worst possible outcome if a prospect tells you no? Your product or service has been rejected, not you. Take it as a professional rejection, not a personal one. After the sales call, rewind the game tape and figure out what you'd do differently next time.

Turn around self-defeating thoughts. Next time your inner voice begins to doubt your skills, stop and write down the defeatist talk going through your head. Seeing it on paper can diminish its power over you, so you can put it into perspective.

Finally, keep score of your successes. While we can't stop the negative thoughts, we can balance them out. Start a success journal, jotting down notes on what worked well in every sales call. Rank the prospect's improved interest level when you used his name, or a new strategy for overcoming a common objection. Just documenting positive outcomes will help put a positive spin on your self-talk.

Remember that most successful people have not only failed, but they are good at failing. They rebound stronger, better equipped to win the next time. They have an authentic appreciation for what they learned from failure.

Take control of your fears by focusing on the prospect who said yes, instead of dwelling on the one who didn't.

GET YOUR MIND RIGHT
BEFORE SELLING

SALES HAS ALWAYS BEEN a psychological game. It always takes skill to close a sale, but half of the battle happens in your head. Too much rejection on any given day can invoke fear in even the most seasoned of sales veterans, deflating their confidence. The trick is to recognize the fear, own up to it quickly and address it before it becomes paralyzing.

If you feel yourself starting to sink, try these strategies for conquering your fears before they drag you down.

First, believe in the product you're selling. If you really believe that the world will be a better place once more people use your products or services, you're halfway to overcoming your fears. After all, if you truly believe in the value of your products or services, you're doing your prospects a disservice by not calling them. If you don't have a strong belief in the products or services you're selling, spend time with someone who has a strong sense of the benefits your business offers prospects. Most owners and founders start a company because they have a strong vision, and they'll almost always be more than happy to share it with you.

Next, make sure you're focused on the activity, not the outcome. Ultimately you don't have complete control over how many of your prospects sign a check.

However, you can control how many sales calls you make a day. If your goal is just to reach a certain level of activity, you can feel successful even when the sale hasn't closed yet. It can also help to identify a partner who will hold you accountable for meeting your prospecting activity targets.

During slow times, prepare by role-playing sales calls, so you can work out any kinks behind the scenes. Preparation leads to confidence; confidence closes sales. Most sales reps understand this, but very few follow through by studying and practicing their playbook regularly.

Find ways to make selling fun by connecting personally with your prospects. Make it a point to identify a unique point of connection with each client, and then send a fun follow-up gift related to that common interest after your first meeting. Not only will this make it easier to get a second meeting, but it can also help lift some of the pressure you feel to close the sale.

Finally, accept that when prospects finally tell you "no," they're giving you a gift. Even though we can all agree that "yes" is the best answer you could get on a sales call, an authoritative "no" is a very close second. After all, if a prospect leaves you in limbo, you're going to end up investing even more time in a relationship that isn't going anywhere. Getting a firm "no" means you can move on to a prospect that has a sincere interest in your company. If you embrace this philosophy, you won't fear rejection. You'll welcome it.

SUCCESS IS ALL IN THE PREP

WHAT SEPARATES the good salesperson from the great one? One over-looked quality is the willingness to invest in preparation, research and planning to prepare for an initial call to a prospect or your first face-to-face meeting.

Too many sales teams dial for dollars, calling as many prospects as they can while using the same canned approach. Why not work smarter instead of harder? Preparation may take time, but it reduces the number of prospects you need to call by increasing your chances of success. Preparation can make all the difference when it comes to getting the meeting or closing the deal.

You have one opportunity to make a good first impression — and unless you have an unlimited supply of strong prospects, you need to nail it every time.

There are obvious research sources available online. Start with the company's website, then look at your contact's LinkedIn, Facebook and Twitter profiles. Try to find personal connections. Think of these connections as possible ice-breakers you'll use to start building rapport with a prospect. For example, you might find a common acquaintance, a cause you're both passionate about, or a school you both attended.

Use these personal connections to come up with a creative approach for landing the meeting. For instance, if you learn through LinkedIn that your prospect is actively involved in a few organizations, you might plan to casually find that individual at that organization's next event. Even better, ask someone you both know to make an introduction.

Uncovering background information about prospects allows you to craft meaningful statements that help them understand why they should care about your products or services. Saying, "I want to tell you about our services" doesn't help prospects understand why they want to hear about your services. If you were a prospect, what would make it difficult to decline a meeting? Once you know the answer to this question, you're well on your way.

After you've landed the meeting, try scripting your opening statement. You should even consider rehearsing it out loud. Make sure you know how you'll open and close the conversation, and focus on three main educational points that you'll explain during the meeting. Develop thoughtful questions to help the prospect realize a need for what you offer, if one authentically exists, of course. You should also know what makes your company different from your competitors, and why that's meaningful to your clients. Anticipate any objections you might face, and make a plan for how to overcome them.

Practicing will help ease your nerves when you're opening the meeting, and this thorough preparation will allow you to adapt to the conversation with greater confidence. If you already have a general plan for what you're intending to say to pitch your products or services when and if the time comes, you can listen more intently to what your prospect says while asking follow-up questions to build rapport.

Even though strategic planning may seem like a big time investment for something as simple as a phone call or sales meeting, just remember that your strategy is what will make you successful.

REACHING THE REAL DECISION MAKER

NOTHING SHORTENS the sales cycle more dramatically than talking to the right person, right off the bat; so, why do sales teams pitch to contacts who aren't the real decision-makers?

Usually, sales teams prioritize the wrong person because of a lack of confidence. After all, the likelihood of outright rejection is greater once you reach the real decision-maker, and no one enjoys rejection. It can also be tougher to get through to the top decision-maker at the company.

My philosophy? You're going to have to pitch to the real decision-maker at some point if you're successful. Wouldn't you prefer a quick response from the real decision maker, even if it's not what you want to hear, instead of working your tail off for months for the same result down the line? Fast decisions allow you to move on to stronger prospects.

Even though it may seem safer to start with a lower-level influencer, there are still big risks to consider. First, each additional approval layer lengthens your sales cycle. The more involved you become with one prospect, the less time you have to focus on other prospects that might be stronger.

More importantly, you'll lose control over your pitch. When you're pitching an influencer, instead of the real decision maker, you are counting on him to land a meeting for you with the real decision-maker. Do you trust that influencer to pitch your products and services as well as you could? Do you really want to rely on someone else to make your pitch? No one can deliver your message — or overcome objections — as well as you can.

If you're ready to step up and make contact with the right decision makers, here are a few tips.

Do your homework. Prepare for the call thoroughly. Know what makes your prospect tick, the name of the gatekeeper you might encounter, the best way to reach out to your prospect, and the most compelling reason your prospect should meet with a stranger. High-level decision makers expect this due diligence.

Warm up the call as much as possible. Identify common acquaintances that can make an introduction for you or provide a reference. LinkedIn can help you find people you both know or identify organizations your prospect cares about. Use that knowledge to your advantage during the call.

Get creative. Instead of the same-old cold call, send a creative, personalized package in advance to increase the likelihood that the prospect will take your call. Use social-media profiles and common acquaintances to discover personal interests that will allow you to customize the package and really knock it out of the park.

Finally, embrace the word "no." Remember that rejection often clears the path to sales success.

COLD CALLING GETS A BAD RAP

COLD CALLING has a bad reputation, and even the best sales teams dread dialing complete strangers. In reality, the make-or-break moment in most cold calls comes in the first 10-20 seconds of the call, beginning when you say your first word and going until the prospect gives you permission to keep talking. If you can make it past those initial choppy waves, it's all smooth sailing from there. How can you calm those waters? Start by breaking down your introduction into three simple steps.

The Greeting: First impressions are formed within the initial eight seconds of engagement, but they're incredibly difficult to change; so those first few words you say matter immensely. Make your opening strong, especially when calling high-level decision makers. Compare these two approaches:

"Hello Mr. Dawson. How are you today? I'm Susan with Designer Pools."

"Ted, this is Susan with Designer Pools."

Do you notice the subtle difference between the two? The second approach gives off more confidence because Susan uses Ted's first name and has a no-nonsense approach. Most importantly, when you're delivering these first few crucial words, don't rush. Rushing can come across as nervous energy, which will diminish your credibility.

The Compelling Reason: Now that you've identified yourself with enough confidence to capture your prospect's attention, offer a compelling reason for continuing to talk with you. You might offer some new information particularly relevant to your prospect, or recount a success you've had with another similar company. Succinctly deliver your reason in no more than three sentences. You might try something like this: "I read about the new apartment development you're breaking ground on next year. We just completed a pool project for a competitor of yours, using an innovative new design technique that cut his installation costs by 20 percent and allowed him to increase rental rates by 10 percent."

The Request to Continue: Once you've piqued your prospect's interest, get permission to continue the conversation. The trick is to get that permission without directly asking. For example, you might say something like this: "I'd love to share more about it, if you have a couple of minutes."

Once you've put all of this together, your conversational starter might sound something like this: "Ted, this is Susan with Designer Pools. (Pause for reaction.) I read about the new apartment development you're breaking ground on next year. Interestingly, we just completed a pool project for a competitor of yours, using an innovative new design technique that cut his installation costs by 20 percent and allowed him to increase rental rates by 10 percent. (Pause for reaction.) I'd love to share more about it, if you have a couple minutes."

Mastering the art of the cold call is as simple as 1, 2, 3.

COLD FEET? HOW TO AVOID COLD-CALLING MISTAKES

PLANNING ISN'T the most glamorous part of cold calling, but it's worth the investment every time. It's always been interesting to me — from a sales psychology perspective — how sales professionals often spend more time fretting about a potential rejection than actually planning for the cold call. Fear can be paralyzing, preventing you from preparing properly and resulting in a strong desire just to get it over with.

However, it shouldn't be surprising that an unplanned approach typically generates a disappointing response. Instead, try to work smarter, not harder. If you plan your cold calls to improve your results, you can easily end up making fewer cold calls in the end.

Begin with determining exactly what you want from the exchange. Do you want to set an appointment, generate a referral or request an introduction? With that knowledge, plan a confident greeting and a compelling reason to talk. Next, seek permission to continue the conversation. Then, once you've made a compelling case for how your prospect can benefit from meeting with you, you've earned the right to suggest a face-to-face meeting.

Script your preliminary conversation as much as possible. Believe that every word matters — because it does. You can lose a prospect's interest in just a few seconds, so every word has to be brimming with potential.

While it may seem counterintuitive, the purpose of a script isn't to read it, word by word, to your prospect. Instead, writing the script makes you more comfortable with your message, so you can ultimately deliver your ideas in an engaging way. Write it down, refine it, and practice it until you're able to deliver your pitch without thinking about it. Becoming comfortable with your delivery will sideline any fears you might have, empowering you to actually listen to your prospect, instead of scrambling to decide what you're going to say next.

While voicemail should generally be avoided where possible, if you must leave one, make sure you've scripted a concise 8- to 14-second message in advance. Resist the temptation to say too much. You only need to pique the prospect's interest enough to take your call the next time. Expecting prospects to call you back, unless you have a strong and relevant point of connection you've alerted them to, isn't realistic generally.

Finally, it's crucial that you have a back-up plan. If your prospect doesn't agree to your first request, what's the next best thing? Don't miss a golden opportunity. For example, if your prospect isn't available to meet with you right away, you might want to request an introduction to another contact within the company. You could also ask if you can stay in touch with the prospect to provide updates on new product developments, or you could invite the prospect to an upcoming workshop hosted by your company. A good back-up plan will allow you to keep in touch, and it's an easy ask.

The cold-calling formula is simple: outline your objectives, script the discussion, rehearse until your pitch is conversational and engaging, and make sure you have a solid back-up plan ready to go.

BREAKING THROUGH THE VOICEMAIL BARRIER

THIRTY YEARS AGO, before caller ID and voicemail, we actually answered our phone to find out who was on the other end. Eek. Gasp. Horror.

Since those days are long behind us, savvy sales teams have learned to view caller ID and voicemail as vital selling tools, not agonizingly restrictive systems used to prevent salespeople from ever reaching a live prospect.

If you're not getting through, there are a few strategies you can use to win the voicemail wars.

Remember that less is more when it comes to leaving a voicemail — keep your message between 8 and 14 seconds. Your message will need to be concise and purposefully crafted to squeeze it into that timeframe. Don't wing it. Script your message, and then leave it in your own voicemail inbox. Listen to it. If you were a prospect, would you return the call?

Speak slowly, with confidence and authority, to make a strong impression. Fast talkers come across as nervous, and they're less influential. Make sure you're avoiding passive phrases such as "I'm just calling to...."

Call the prospect by his first name only for a more personal message, and then provide a meaningful reason that your prospect can benefit from talking with you. Use the power of suggestion to your advantage. For example, you could say, "We have a mutual friend, Bob, who suggested we connect. We've put some creative strategies in place at his operation, which are driving significant revenue. Let's talk to see if we can do the same for you." Don't say too much. Your objective is simply to pique your prospect's interest enough to take your call the next time. If you give away your whole pitch, you risk giving your recipient a reason not to meet with you.

Increasingly challenged to get more done, successful business people must prioritize the calls they'll return, so when they don't call you back, don't take it personally. In fact, unless you have a strong existing relationship, you should assume they won't. Instead, think of your message as the very first step in the effort to land a meeting. If you have a strong case study outlining how you've helped similar companies, mention in your message that you'll be sending it for review prior to your next call; then give a specific timeframe when you'll call back.

Before you call, know what your next steps should be. Consider leaving three messages with different content three business days apart, supplemented with email or direct mail, to impress upon the prospect that you're persistent but not aggressive.

Voicemail doesn't have to be a dead end. Demonstrate you have value to offer, and you'll ultimately break through the voicemail barrier.

COLD EMAIL MASTERY, A CLICK AWAY FROM ANYONE

IF EXECUTED WELL, email can significantly improve your engagement rate, even with otherwise cold prospects — at least according to Scott Britton with Life-longlearner.com, the forensic accountant of the email world whose company was acquired by Constant Contact for $100 million in 2012.

If you know the name of a targeted company, but don't have the decision-maker's name or email address, your search should start on LinkedIn. Use the Advanced Search feature to look for the department and title of the decision maker at your targeted company. You could get a number of results, so to narrow down the list, look for "implicit signals," says Britton, by looking closely at endorsements. What skills is your decision-maker most likely to have?

If your prospect's title and job description are both vague, review his profile for prior positions. After all, most professionals tend to stay within their chosen fields. If you see a consistent track record of relevant leadership, you've likely found your prospect, even if his current title is simply a generic "VP."

Read through the recommendations to further validate you have the decision maker. You should also see how other people address this individual. If his name is Matthew, but colleagues call him "Matt" in their recommendations, use Matt in your emails so that you don't call attention to your lack of familiarity with him.

Now that you have the prospect's name, it's time to find the email address. There are a handful of popular formulas most companies use to construct employee email addresses:

firstinitial+lastname@companyname.com
lastname@companyname.com
firstname@companyname.com
firstname+lastname@companyname.com
firstinitial+lastinitial@companyname.com

The website mailtester.com allows you to enter each of your suggested email addresses and verify the addresses. If the email address does exist, a green box pops up saying that the email address exists on the server. If it's not a valid email address, then a red box will pop up stating that the address does not exist on the server.

If you're still coming up short, search Google for your prospect's Twitter handle, then visit Snapbird.org to search that person's Twitter history for key-words such as "email me," "contact me," or the company's website domain, which likely makes up the last part of that person's email address and might just help you stumble upon it. Twitter will scour the archives for conversations featuring those keywords — tweets where your prospect might have shared his email address publicly.

Use these unique techniques for identifying a high-value prospect's name and email address, and you're likely to find success most of the time.

THE OPPORTUNITY IN 'NO'

WHEN YOUR BUSINESS is young, you naturally welcome every new customer with open arms so you can find your footing, but too many business owners have trouble breaking that pattern even after their businesses are more established. If the "say yes to everything" mentality trickles down to the front line sales team, it can be a serious problem. If you're not careful, this can even be a death sentence to your business.

What if you could tell a prospective customer no, and actually make more money than if you'd agreed to the partnership? If you're a service provider, then that is likely the case more often than you realize.

Customers that aren't a good fit can be a drain on your team, your reputation and ultimately, your profitability. However, you must be proactively seeking out ideal customers, not simply reacting exclusively to inbound prospects, to be able to say no with confidence. A good balance of inbound and outbound prospecting activity is essential for the health of your business.

Empowering your team to more carefully scrutinize new customers starts with defining the characteristics of a great customer. Great customers vary by business, but your definition could start by including an assessment of cultural fit, whether you can make a real difference for this customer, whether the work you'll do for this prospective customer leverages your organization's strongest assets, and whether you'll be paid fairly for your team's efforts.

Next, determine what qualifying questions you'll consistently ask prospects to determine if they're a good fit for your firm, and provide those questions to your entire sales team. If your sales team is on the fence about a prospective customer after an initial qualifying interview, encourage the team to debrief the opportunity with other colleagues for a gut check.

When you do need to decline work from a prospective customer, doing so with grace will lead to respect in the marketplace. However, never burn a bridge. Help your prospect see why a different company might be a better fit for his current needs. Offer specific companies that you'd recommend. Consider going above and beyond by making an initial introduction to another business.

Saying no doesn't have to end the relationship. If you handle this interaction with kindness and assist the prospect in finding a more suitable partner, you'll benefit from referrals and positive word of mouth — and who knows, there may come a time down the road when that same prospect is a good fit for your company after all.

SIX BEST PRACTICES TO BOOST SALES EFFICIENCY

THOMAS WATSON, President of IBM in the fifties, insightfully declared, "Nothing happens until a sale is made." A company's sales effort is the ultimate driver of organizational growth. It is the most critical function within any company and requires advanced training and intestinal fortitude for success.

Since the sales profession is not for everyone, when you construct a winning sales team, allow the team to do what it does best with limited distractions for maximum efficiency. While this may seem controversial, the rest of the organization should consider it a top priority to support the sales team. Dedicated salespeople should only do one thing — sell. Allow others within your firm to take care of related administrative, marketing and operational tasks so that your sales professionals may spend most all of their time making contact with prospects.

Beyond allowing the sales team to focus, implement these five sales-efficiency best practices in order to boost performance.

Ensure that sales reps are given quality leads. Asking them to scrub or quality check the data is detracting from vital selling time. If your sales team is charged with generating leads, be sure to coach on how to identify ideal prospects, as well as how to avoid wasting time on bad leads.

Organize leads into groups according to similar business category, lead source, title of prospect or company size. This will allow your sales team to prepare for calls more efficiently by letting the team analyze the entire group at once, instead of preparing for one call at a time. This will also give your team the ability to easily customize messaging and engage targeted prospects more effectively.

Establish a consistent, disciplined prospecting process — a specific sequence of calls, emails and/or direct mail that works — eliminating as many options as you can. Many studies correlate sales-process structure with sales efficiency and, ultimately, with results. Narrow the lead list or territory to ensure it's manageable for each sales rep. Create targets for the number of completed calls and meetings each week. Craft discussion guides and templates to streamline this process. This uniformity will allow sales management to see patterns, opportunities for sales-process improvement, and strategies for reducing the length of the sales cycle.

A disciplined process can only be effective if you have the time management skills to execute it. Block time on your calendar for each planned prospecting activity, instead of approaching each day with no plan. Unless you have a plan, low-priority tasks will dominate your schedule.

Every time a sale is closed, make it a standard to request at least three referrals from that satisfied customer. Referrals can be an infinite source of warm leads.

Whether you are a sales rep or sales manager, consistently applying these simple best practices in sales efficiency will inevitably boost sales performance.

EIGHT-SECOND RULE OF FIRST IMPRESSIONS

EIGHT SECONDS is not only the length of a successful bull ride, it's also how long we have to leave a first impression on those we meet. For bull riders, that eight seconds is an eternity — but for the rest of us, it's gone in the mere blink of an eye.

In the first eight seconds after meeting a prospect, the prospect evaluates your social standing. If the prospect thinks you have comparable business or social standing, you'll be considered a possible partner. If you appear to have a higher status, you'll be admired, and your prospect will cultivate a relationship with you, since you'll be seen as a valuable contact. If the prospect thinks you're at a lower social level, though, you'll be kept at arm's length.

It's a harsh reality, but we have to accept it. Once a first impression is formed, it's extraordinarily difficult to change it, so it's crucial that you put your best foot forward all the time. Not only is it essential to master the art of the first impression in sales, but it's also an important life skill.

While you can't completely predict what kind of first impression you'll make, there are at least eight factors you can control.

One picture is worth a thousand words. When your prospects think of you, what do they picture? Dressing up more than expected can help accentuate your high standing. Pay attention to the details. Carry a nice leather portfolio, instead of a free canvas portfolio with someone else's logo. Don't let papers fall out in a disorganized way. Less is more. Invest in a nice pen, not a disposable plastic pen that's seen better days. Ladies, leave the giant purse in the car.

When you see your prospects enter the room, stand and walk to greet them, instead of waiting for them to walk to you. If you wait, you could come off as passive or unsure.

Memorize your opening line. Make sure you have a point of connection ready to pull from your arsenal, like a common acquaintance or shared interest.

Carry yourself with confidence and genuine enthusiasm. Weakness may be a repellent, but arrogance can be even worse. Find the middle ground.

Don't fidget. Avoid nervous tie adjustments, touching your watch (which insinuates you're in a hurry), shaking your leg or fiddling with your pen.

Smile, and make eye contact. We are naturally attracted to those who smile, and eye contact demonstrates confidence.

Stay focused. Tune out everything, staying completely attentive to your prospect. Avoid the temptation to glance away when someone walks by. Turn your cell phone off, and make sure it's out of sight.

Your handshake should be firm, of course. Don't shake like a dead fish, or a bone crusher. Avoid the two-handed shake or pulling the prospect closer while you shake hands. Some other handshakes to avoid are the political handshake, where your other hand is placed on the prospect's forearm or shoulder, and the cupped shake, where your palm doesn't touch your prospect's palm, which could make the prospect think you're shy — or even hiding something.

Leave the prospect with a sense of your competence, preparedness and likability by making a good first impression, and you're on your way to a successful sale.

THE SECRET OF INSTANT RAPPORT

REGARDLESS OF THE STRENGTH of the sales pitch, or even the quality of the products and services, the reality is that people buy from those they like and trust. The challenge for sales professionals is to master the art of instant rapport with someone you may be meeting for the very first time, instead of leaving it to chance.

What is rapport? It's the point at which your prospects understand you and believe that you understand them. The majority of buying decisions are made primarily for emotional reasons, including feelings of trust and rapport. Once these intangible feelings are in play, most prospects will seek out rational justification for the emotional decisions they've already made. Without rapport, many buyers feel so uncomfortable that they aren't likely to buy — even if they really want the product.

When meeting a prospect for the first time, remember that most first impressions are made within eight seconds. Walk toward your prospect assertively, offering your hand. Make sure you're dressed one step above what prospects might expect, so that your prospects immediately see you as a valuable business partner.

Kick off the conversation with open-ended, rapport-building questions designed to help you understand your prospect better. Don't talk too much about yourself. Remember that dominating the conversation is the quickest way to derail rapport. Demonstrate active listening skills by making regular eye contact, taking notes, avoiding distractions, repeating what you heard and asking thoughtful follow-up questions.

Research shows that 70 to 90 percent of communication is non-verbal. If your prospect's body language doesn't align with what he is saying, trust his body language. Ask questions to uncover why the prospect may be hesitant.

You can also use body language to communicate that you think like your prospect by mirroring and matching nonverbal cues. If your prospect is leaning forward intently, you should lean forward, too. If your prospect is gesturing widely when she talks, match her style. Match your prospect's tone and tempo as well. For example, if your prospect speaks quickly, pick up your pace. While this can certainly be overdone, and your synchronization should be subtle, mirroring and matching your prospect's non-verbal hints will make that person feel connected to you.

In the end, confidence can lead to rapport. During your very first conversation with your prospect, act like you already have a rapport. If you talk with prospects as if they are already close friends you care about, you are more likely to break down barriers and create a connection quickly.

BUILDING TRUST IN SALES

EVEN THOUGH you will need to identify your prospect's needs before you make a successful sale, your knowledge won't mean much if your relationship with the prospect isn't built on trust.

Smart buyers are generally willing to consider the guidance of salespeople, but only if trust has been established first. Once a prospect trusts the seller, the first — and arguably hardest — step to success is out of the way.

How do you build trust with a prospect? First, prove that you are trustworthy. How can you show that you are accountable, credible and authentic? Good listening skills can go a long way. Make sure that you are dependable, too. Buyers want to know that you mean what you say. Don't promise buyers the moon, only to fall short.

Prove that you're competent by being an expert. Be bold, but don't just sell the hype. Big slogans and proclamations are nice, but if there isn't substance, you will undermine any trust you've built. Of course, salespeople are in the business of shining the best possible light on a service, so most prospects have learned to be skeptical. Sellers have to be able to answer to that skepticism, so they have to know every aspect of their products or services. Don't be caught off guard by questions about your product or your competition.

You also need to be knowledgeable about your prospect's business, his competitors and the marketplace, the needs of his customers, and how your product can help address those needs. Be able to identify the return on investment for buying your product. You should be prepared with concrete examples of results and client testimonials, which show a track record of integrity.

Demonstrate your integrity by showing the customer you have his best interests at heart, even if that means sending him to a competitor when what you are offering isn't quite right at that time. Taking a selfless approach could drive future business and referrals more than anything you can say.

Unless you have already built a relationship with the prospect, most new buyers have no reason to trust you. They don't know you, and they aren't familiar with how you have helped others find success. Get personal with your prospects by letting them into your world, and showing them what matters to you. Help your prospects understand there is a real person behind the products or services you are selling.

Don't take trust for granted. Even after you have built a basic foundation of trust, you need to keep building trust in each of your early conversations before you can cross the bridge that leads to a solid, long-standing partnership.

THE MORE YOU TELL, THE LESS YOU SELL

IN SEVEN HABITS OF HIGHLY EFFECTIVE PEOPLE, Stephen Covey wrote, "Seek first to understand, then to be understood." This principle alone has the power to solve an industry-wide sales challenge: underdeveloped listening skills.

In today's Information Age, prospective customers often come to the table armed with enough facts to make their own logical decisions. However, most of us make our decisions emotionally first, often based on how much we trust the salesperson. Because of this fact, salespeople have to be more than information providers. Instead, they have to focus on building relationships — but before you can build the foundation for any good relationship, you have to listen.

For sales teams trained under the old sales model, this transition can be challenging. Instead of just outlining features and benefits, they have to dedicate most of their time to asking high-impact, open-ended questions, and then listening carefully. After all, we do have two ears and just one mouth for a reason.

Better listening skills don't just help sales teams build stronger relationships and close more sales; listening carefully also helps your sales team become more efficient with their prospecting. By listening more — and talking less —

they can quickly distinguish between good prospects and dead ends, avoiding time-killers and moving on to stronger possibilities.

If you want to sharpen your listening skills, start by avoiding these common pitfalls: Resist the temptation to focus so much on what you're going to say next that you're not hearing what the prospect is telling you. Avoid making assumptions, answering questions that haven't been asked, or solving problems that haven't been articulated. Derailing the conversation is a clear sign that you aren't listening to your prospect. If you switch subjects too quickly, your prospect will know you're not really listening. Placating prospects by agreeing with almost everything they say often comes across as self-serving, and working too hard to prove you have the solution to all the problems your prospects mention will come across as insincere.

Remember that emotions drive purchases more than intellect, so don't underestimate the importance of building rapport by asking thoughtful questions that encourage your prospects to articulate their needs. You won't close sales by telling prospects what their problems are. Ask leading questions that allow prospects to realize their needs in their own way.

Next, ask meaningful follow-up questions. For example, when you hear your prospect identify a source of pain, you could say, "Tell me how much this problem is costing you." You will also want to restate what you've heard occasionally, to show you're paying attention. Finally, recognize that a brief pause is a powerful tool for bringing out information a prospect may have never intended to share.

Developing better listening skills takes discipline, but it can pay out big dividends.

DON'T LET ZEAL KILL THE SALE

PASSION IS A VITAL SKILL for entrepreneurs, but it can actually kill a sales call. While it may seem counterintuitive, being overzealous can simply overwhelm a prospect.

Asking for the sale is an essential selling skill, but before you have earned the right to ask, you have to focus on building trust with your prospect. Sales is a process, and not just a question. If your enthusiasm gets the better of you, and you ask too soon, you'll certainly get an answer — but it won't be the one you want.

Passion could also make you rush through the all-important needs assessment, when you should be asking high-impact questions that get your prospects talking about their needs. Guide your prospects through those discussions properly, and your buyers will realize that they need your products or services on their own. However, if you make assumptions about what your prospects need, instead of letting them get there on their own, you risk losing the sale.

More importantly, if you cut the needs assessment short by jumping on the very first need your prospects divulge, you may miss additional opportunities to sell even more. Make sure you explore your prospects' needs before offering solutions. Once you shift the focus away from exploring those needs, it can be challenging to get your potential buyer to go back.

Passion can also cause you to talk too much in a sales conversation. Successful sales people only talk 20 percent of the time. If you truly want to understand and relate to your prospect's concerns, you'll need to set your passion aside so you can improve your likelihood of closing the sale.

Once a prospect begins to demonstrate buying signals, don't oversell. Passionate people often try to make every point they had originally outlined, even after the prospect has clearly made a buying decision. If you're not careful, you might talk your prospect out of the sale. Once your prospect is ready to buy, focus on closing the sale.

While you still want your passion to show, make sure you stay focused on the needs of your prospects. After all, passion can propel you to the top, but it can also send you right over the cliff.

THE POWER OF QUESTIONS

LET'S FACE IT. Many people don't have a positive reaction to the word "sales." It's often associated with old-style, won't-take-no-for-an-answer tactics that involve selling a product or service even when it's not right for the customer.

Consultative selling is much more effective. Some call it needs-based or strategic selling. This method's success hinges on one simple yet often overlooked fact: There is no basis for a sale until you solve a problem.

With this approach, the salesperson works as consultant, uncovering each customer's needs and pains. Provided the sales rep's products or services are indeed a good fit for that prospect, the rep then tailors his sales pitch to explain how so. It's all about personalizing your messages to meet a specific prospect's actual, self-identified needs.

While this approach can certainly accelerate sales, the challenge is to keep quiet until you really know what the prospect needs. Because the prospect's needs are at the heart of the consultative-sales process, the most important component of a sales meeting is the needs assessment, where you ask a series of thoughtful, open-ended questions designed to uncover your prospect's deeper needs and buying motives.

Even if that sounds easy at first, it's not. Consultative selling is an art form, and like any art, mastery takes time. You need to ask precisely the right questions, in the right order to succeed. You have to listen intently, modifying your questions to suit each individual prospect.

Your questions should almost always be open-ended, so that you can keep the prospect talking 80 percent of the time. Remember that a talkative prospect is the telltale sign of a good sales call.

Start by asking the prospect to tell you about a particular aspect of his business. If you're selling financial planning services, you might ask questions like these:

"How do you think a successful relationship with a financial planner would look?" Prospects answering this question may give you insight into the benefits of your product or service that speak most deeply to their own needs.

"How often does your current financial planner meet with you, and what do you see as the most valuable aspect of those meetings?" You might uncover a desire to see more of the planner or for more substance during meetings, which you could emphasize in your pitch.

"What's worked well with financial planners you've used in the past? What could have been better?" Questions like these are nice, low-key ways of revealing the prospect's pain points with your competitors.

"What would it take for you to give our company a shot at your business?" This is a great wrap-up question because, if your prospect answers candidly, he is handing you a formula for securing his business.

Whether you are a salesperson or the CEO, mastering the power of questioning will serve you well for a lifetime. Not only will you close more business, but you will also make your customers feel understood and respected.

HOW TO ASK THE TOUGH QUESTIONS

THE WORLD'S BEST SALESPEOPLE excel at asking engaging questions and actively listening to a prospect's response without interruption. They master the art of posing high-impact questions that generate insightful responses which offer a glimpse into a prospect's decision-making process, competitors also under consideration, the likelihood of purchase, or even the factors that will be weighed most heavily by decision makers.

Prospects are generally amenable to answering the predictable questions related to business challenges they are facing or experiences with past products or services, but discomfort can creep into your prospect meeting when more challenging questions are asked, if you haven't first earned the right to ask those questions.

So what does it mean to "earn the right" to ask tough questions? It means you must build trust before probing into the soul of your prospect. Do this by demonstrating good listening skills showing your integrity by citing examples illustrating how you have customers' best interests at heart, proving competence in what you're selling, and showing you trust your prospect by giving a bit of insight into what makes you tick.

Once trust is built, how do you ask the tough questions? Sometimes it means warming a prospect up to the topic. If your goal is to determine if the prospect really intends to buy from you, begin asking preliminary closing questions throughout your conversation, such as "Can you see this service being valuable to your team?" and "Does this sound like a service in which you'd be interested in investing?"

There are other questions that just need to be asked directly, with eye contact and without wavering or fidgeting, as though you ask these every single day from prospects that are more than happy to address them with you. These might include topics such as budget, influencers involved in the purchase decision, who has the ability to sign a contract, and a request for an introduction to that person.

If you are feeling uneasy about asking challenging questions, reflect on why. With most sales reps, it's due to hope or fear. As long as you don't ask tough questions that could result in a "no," you can continue to hope that your efforts will result in a sale, despite the reality of the situation. You may also be fearful that despite all of your best efforts, your prospect still isn't interested in buying from you. And asking tough questions may require you to face that inevitable "no" before you're ready.

Hope and fear are just a recipe for wasted effort. Stop wasting your time and your prospects' time. Ask the tough questions as soon as you've built enough trust to do so, and focus on prospects that can truly benefit from your unique offering.

MASTERING THE PERFECT PITCH

DELIVERING THE PERFECT SALES PITCH is like throwing a no-hitter. It's no easy feat, but those who have mastered the art of the flawless pitch have the power to consistently bring home more wins.

In reality, every salesperson gives several sales pitches before closing a sale. For example, you might deliver an elevator pitch over the phone to secure a sales meeting, but you'll need a second pitch for a one-on-one sales conversation with the prospective buyer, or possibly a more formal sales pitch presentation to a group of buyers and influencers. Presenting your pitch to a group is the most challenging scenario because the formality of the situation can limit your innate ability to engage prospects and build rapport.

It's been my experience that salespeople who just deliver presentations, sans engagement, endure long sales cycles and low close rates. On the other hand, when a salesperson involves prospects through a more interactive, engaging demonstration, that percentage jumps significantly.

How can you create an engaging, interactive demonstration?

Show passion. Undeniable passion closes sales. It's contagious, and prospects love it.

Don't just tell your prospects about your products or service; show them the difference you've made for other clients. Offer facts and examples to prove you've successfully resolved the type of pain your prospect is experiencing. Leading with results can convince prospects that you have the right solution to meet their needs, even without a direct sales pitch.

Communicate instead of lecturing. Step away from your PowerPoint. Lay down the clicker. Look your prospects in the eyes, and have a heart-to-heart about a topic that's important to them. Ask for their perspective. You'll be remembered for connecting with them personally.

Identify their pain, and then speak directly to their concerns. Be sure you know what pain your prospects are experiencing that led them to consider your proposal. If you can't gather this information in advance, build a quick needs assessment conversation into your pitch, and then adapt your presentation on the fly.

Demonstrate you care about your prospect's company and his goals. Your delivery should feel personal.

If a prospect asks you a direct question, answer directly. In the sales world, candor is refreshing. There's no faster way to earn a prospect's respect than by answering the tough questions directly, even when the answer isn't easy.

Rehearse so you can confidently own the room. Being completely familiar with your presentation will give you the confidence to go off script. Don't ever read from the screen. Reading from the screen makes you seem unprepared, and if you can't keep eye contact, you'll seem less confident.

Quickly make it clear what the prospect can get out of a partnership with your company, and stay focused on what benefits he can look forward to receiving. Spend 80 percent of your time talking about your prospect's needs, not your own products or services.

Like every major league pitcher, a salesperson must honestly assess his current skill level and dedicate time to developing those skills in order to find his way to the perfect pitch and that coveted no-hitter.

TALK LIKE TED
IN YOUR SALES PITCH

TED IS A NONPROFIT committed to spreading ideas in the form of succinct yet powerful talks that are all 18 minutes or less. TED Talks have a distinct style that results in spectacularly high levels of viewer engagement. This style is predicated on several principles guiding TED Talk presenters, as outlined by Carmine Gallo in "Talk Like TED."

Interestingly, these principles can just as easily be applied to a sales pitch as to a keynote. In fact, using these TED presentation tips will not only grow the relationship you have already with your prospect, but you will also close more business.

Gallo begins by pointing out that "passion is contagious." Help your audience members understand why you believe passionately in what you do, and they're more likely to trust you. Prospects make buying decisions first based on emotion, and then they seek the rational justification for decisions they've made. Once an emotional connection has been established, based on your passion, anything you say next has immediate credibility.

It's hard for people to engage if they can't relate to what you're saying, and stories are a powerful way to connect. If you "master the art of storytelling," your prospects will understand your key ideas even better. Next time you make a pitch, incorporate a well-placed story that reinforces your brand's primary differentiators. Make your story so rich with details that your prospect can imagine being with you at the time.

Be ready to lead a conversation with your prospect. Prepare extensively for your sales meeting, but in the moment, focus on just having an honest conversation with your prospect, instead of anticipating what you're going to say next.

If you want your pitch to stand out from your competitors and remain on the mind of your prospect well after your sales meeting, Gallo recommends that you "deliver jaw-dropping moments." Include an unexpected or shocking statistic. Use props or a demo to showcase your offering. Incorporate pictures and video to reinforce your point.

Finally, you should "lighten up." Sales meetings are usually pretty predictable. Combine humor and a bit of novelty to make your audience more receptive to your message and to build rapport. Don't tell knock-knock jokes, but you should remember not to take yourself too seriously. Consider a funny anecdote, personal story or observation related to your message, or share a funny analogy or metaphor.

There's nothing like watching a TED Talk to see how to apply these principles. For a little inspiration, visit www.ted.com and search for "How Schools Kill Creativity." You'll see an everyday guy, Ken Robinson, delivering the most persuasive, mind-shaping presentation of his life.

USE STORYTELLING TO SWAY CUSTOMERS

THERE IS PERHAPS no greater weapon in a salesperson's arsenal than a great story. There are fundamental selling skills salespeople must have to find success, like how to uncover a prospect's needs, formulate customized solutions, overcome objections and ask for the business. You would assume having these skills, along with the proper selling tools and training, would always lead to success. Why then do so many sales professionals fail to close consistently?

Often, the missing link is the intangible ability to connect with a prospect in a meaningful way. One way to build trust is to share powerful, engaging stories.

It may be easy to tell a prospect how your product or service is different, but if you can bring those differentiators to life through inspiring, practiced storytelling, your prospects are much more likely to relate — and to remember. Sharing how you've gone above and beyond for a specific customer, for example, gives your prospects a chance to picture themselves as part of your story.

Storytelling is a powerful technique for delivering complex information in a way that builds an emotional connection with your audience. If you're not sure which stories should make the cut, there are five kinds of stories every salesperson should have in his pocket.

Paint a picture of your unequivocal commitment to your customers, showing that your clients aren't just stepping stones on the way to reaching your sales target.

Share your subject-matter expertise. For example, you could tell a story about a client with flat sales and customer attrition, outlining how you were able to turn it around with relative ease.

Use stories to demonstrate your willingness to partner with your clients to find unique solutions that get the job done. Consider sharing an anecdote about how your entire team worked all weekend long at no additional cost to the client to make sure a project was completed on time.

Tell a story to showcase your ability to communicate clearly and frequently with clients, so there aren't any surprises.

Lastly, there's nothing better than a story to reveal your company's integrity.

The formula for telling a memorable story is to organize it with a clear beginning, middle and end. Start by telling your prospects what you're about to prove. Use transition words such as "first," "next" and "finally" to help organize the story in their minds. Evoke emotion at pivotal points in the story. Like the most powerful prose, end where you began by restating what you've just proven.

Once you've unleashed the power of your own storytelling abilities, consider using this skill outside the sales process, too. Stories are powerful tools for motivating prospects, but they also allow your team and outside influencers to see just what makes your company so unique.

TECHNIQUES FOR REVEALING HIDDEN OBJECTIONS

IT SOMETIMES SEEMS like prospects speak their own language. You might think it's positive when your prospect says, "Call me back in a few months." However, more often, your prospect is actually saying, "You can try, but you'll be screened by my gatekeeper relentlessly."

Prospects don't intentionally speak in code, but when they're anxious about telling you the truth, they will stall. If you want to make progress, you have to dig deep to get to the heart of the objection. After all, you can't overcome an objection if you're never given the chance.

If your prospect is stalling, there are a few techniques you can try to get to the root of his objection.

For example, your prospect might say, "I'm happy with our current provider." If you want to get around this objection, try saying, "It sounds like you have a long-lasting relationship. Tell me more about what's working with that relationship." Next, ask what could be better, opening the door to sell the value of change.

Maybe your prospect is saying, "Send me more information." Instead of sending the information right away, consider saying, "Let's talk more about your process, so I can make sure I'm sending you the most meaningful information. Based on our discussion today, do you think our products or services could offer a strong value to your organization?" Next, ask who would be involved in the decision-making process, the criteria that will be used, and how the information you'll send will inform the consideration process. If your prospect answers all of these questions, there's a good chance that he is getting ready to make a commitment.

Prospects often stall by saying, "I need to think it over." If your prospect needs to think about it, you could say, "That makes perfect sense. This is an important decision that could create significant opportunity for your business. Tell me more about what's causing your hesitation."

Sometimes prospects defer to others by saying, "I need to talk it over with my boss." If your prospect is passing the buck, say, "I can certainly understand the desire for a collaborative decision-making process. Tell me more about your boss's role in this decision. Do you think your boss will see the value here, like you do? What questions will your boss have for me?" Walking through these questions will help your prospect persuade others in the organization, but ideally, your prospect will see that there's a need for your presence in the meeting.

Finally, many prospects will hint at a restrictive budget by saying, "I'll have to look at the numbers." If your prospect is overly conscious of budget, consider saying, "I'm hearing some hesitation about the budget. Talk to me about what's causing your concerns." You may not have created enough perceived value to warrant the expense. Once you've heard out the prospect, begin to build additional value before asking for the sale again.

Once your prospect reveals his true objection, always paraphrase what you heard, validate the concern, and overcome it. For example, you could reaffirm your value proposition, showing that the value outweighs your prospect's concerns. You could also outline the costs associated with not moving forward quickly. Finally, you could adjust your offer to address the prospect's uncovered need.

Keep the lines of conversation open, and you'll easily break the prospect code.

HANDLING THOSE OBJECTIONS

NOW I MAY BE WIRED differently than most people, but I actually look forward to hearing objections on a sales call. Why? Each objection is a clue. My prospects might want me to slow down; they might need me to provide more information; or they may just need me to make them feel more confident about the purchase. No matter how you slice it, though, the beauty of an objection is that it means the prospect is listening and engaged.

The first step in overcoming objections is to confirm how serious they are. Oftentimes, early objections are simply a knee-jerk reaction. Resist fanning a minor objection into a raging inferno due to your assumptions, perceptions and emotions. Control the fire by acknowledging the objection and attempting to move past it.

For example, if you're cold calling a small-business owner to book an appointment, and your prospect says, "We don't have the budget for your services." Your response might be, "I understand completely. That's an issue for most small businesses. The reason for my call is to see if we can actually save you money — dollars you could put towards other improvements." If your prospect restates the objection, you know that it's likely significant and not simply a diversionary tactic to get off the phone.

Try these strategies for overcoming serious objections.

Complement It: Most people use the direct approach for overcoming objections, explaining what they heard and why it isn't accurate. If you take this approach, you have to be careful not to come across as argumentative. Instead, disarm your prospect and differentiate yourself from the competition by explaining how what you offer can complement what he already has in place, instead of replacing it entirely. For example, your prospect might say, "We use your competitor and are satisfied." You could respond, "I'm glad you already see the value in this service. Many of my clients find that our service complements those of our competitors. Let's discuss how."

Prevent It: Every salesperson worth his salt can anticipate common objections. Why not eliminate them by addressing objections before they're raised? If a common concern is return on investment, strike preemptively like this: "Given the fluctuating economy, small-business owners like you have to scrutinize every investment's return. We'll realize a minimum ROI of 25 percent within three months. Let's talk about how we can do that."

Convert to a Trial Close: When you already have several points of agreement with the prospect and you're getting buying signals, isolate the main objection and propose a sale if you can reach an acceptable solution. For example, your prospect might say, "I need to wait 90 days before incurring any additional expenses." You could answer, "Great! So, if I understand you correctly, if we can delay the timing, I have your commitment to move forward."

Peel the Onion: The toughest objection of all is when your prospect says, "I'll have to think about it." It signals that you haven't built enough trust and rapport for the prospect to reveal the real objection. Before you give up, try asking for the objection. It shows that you are genuinely interested in learning about the prospect's needs. For example, try saying, "I can certainly understand that. This is a big decision, and I want you to feel completely comfortable. Tell me more about what's causing your hesitation."

Next time a prospect objects, thank him for telling you where he stands, and then use these tips to get the conversation back on the path to success.

SURE-FIRE WAYS TO OVERCOME PRICE OBJECTIONS

HOW MANY TIMES have you heard a prospect ask, "Can you do it for less?" While this kind of question sometimes signals a serious concern about the price tag, it's also possible that your prospect is simply negotiating out of habit. Just because a prospect asks whether or not you could lower your price doesn't mean he is prepared to walk away if you don't. In fact, objections to your pricing may really signal other concerns that are masquerading in disguise.

If you aren't sure whether the prospect's supposed sticker shock is a smoke screen or a legitimate concern, ask your prospect to explain his objection in more detail. For example, you might say, "Tell me more about your concern." After you've heard your prospect out, make sure that your prospect has all his cards on the table by asking, "Do you have other concerns?" Once everything is out in the open, you can move forward without feeling like you're walking through a minefield.

You may find that your prospect's initial financial concerns are masking the fact that he has to consult with the real decision maker, which he may have failed to share with you; or maybe he has a personal friendship with a vendor that would make change uncomfortable. Tackle these kinds of hidden objections first, and you may not have to lower your price.

However, if you feel certain that price is the only remaining objection, try asking your prospect, "If I overcome your price concerns, are you ready to move forward?" This prevents your prospect from raising another objection after you've dealt fairly with the price issue.

Then try these four strategies for overcoming the price objection.

Objections to price often mean you haven't done a good job of selling the value of your products or services. Reiterate the prospect's needs, and then put a value on overcoming these business problems, including any opportunity costs related to making a slow decision.

If your prospect isn't confident that your products or services will perform, share case studies of how you generated the projected outcome for similar companies, including testimonials. Consider offering a money-back guarantee if you don't meet performance metrics.

If your prospect tries to compare you to your competitors, help your prospect understand that he would never ask his primary-care physician to perform heart surgery or hire a cardiologist to treat a cold. While they're both doctors, they offer dramatically different services — like you and your competitors. Unless you're selling a pure commodity, price comparisons between you and your competitors aren't "apples to apples."

As a last resort, negotiate with your prospect but avoid haggling. You should always have a justifiable reason to discount that you share with your prospect, other than simply that the prospect has asked for it, or you risk damaging the integrity of your brand. Those justifiable reasons might include: a reduction in the scope of services, when customers purchase in volume, when they pay quickly, when they have referred several new customers, or if the likelihood for future business is high as a result of entering a new market or capturing a marquee client.

In the end, you have to know your company's value, own it, and help your prospect see it so you can feel confident sticking to your guns.

SIX TIPS FOR SHORTENING THE SALES CYCLE

SALES CAREERS aren't for the faint of heart. You need a dogged sense of determination, you need to be thick-skinned in the face of adversity, and you must be prepared to spend some long days in the pursuit of the almighty sale. I have an incredible respect for sales professionals, so I've dedicated much of my career to helping them work smarter to close sales more efficiently, and the fastest way to do just that is by shortening the sales cycle.

If you don't already know the length of your sales cycle, average the length of time it typically takes you to close a sale — all the way from your first point of contact to a signed order. By shortening this cycle, you have the ability to call on more prospects, ultimately leading to more wins on the scoreboard. Shortened sales cycles also reduce the likelihood of obstacles getting in your way, like more influencers introduced into the sales process — or your prospect simply losing a sense of urgency over time.

More often than not, it's the salesperson that creates the long sales cycle, not the prospect. Follow these tips to ensure you keep things moving:

The easiest way to shorten your sales cycles is to start with the actual decision maker right out of the gate, so determine who controls the company's pocketbook for your product or service before calling. If you're unsure, begin at the very top. It's easy to work your way back down, but it's much harder to travel up.

Get to know your prospect's needs and desires quickly. Don't just assume that he can benefit from what you're selling. Instead of trying to convince a prospect he needs your services, move on to prospects that clearly do.

Deal with known objections early on in your conversation. By dealing with them early, you allow your prospect to focus on how to actually do business with you, instead of why they shouldn't.

Make it easy for your prospect to buy by offering a small trial-run type purchase, instead of asking him to bite off the entire enchilada before you've had an opportunity to prove your worth.

Set your prospect's mind at ease by offering customer testimonials and case studies. You could even offer reviews of your competitors found on third-party review sites to help differentiate your products or services.

And lastly, once you have a prospect's interest, follow up promptly. Find reasons to stay top of mind by adding value and advancing the sale. For example, instead of calling just to "check in," send an article about a recent trend in your prospect's industry; then explain how your product or service can help him leverage that trend to generate results.

If you use all of these tips, you'll find your sales cycle picking up the pace in no time.

BE A SELLER, NOT A BEGGAR

PICTURE THIS: You deliver a great sales pitch. Your prospect gives you strong buying signals. As the meeting ends, your prospect says that he is likely to move forward and will call in a couple days to finalize things. Swoosh! Nothing but net!

You leave on top of the world — but then days pass without a call. A week later, you are calling your prospect and not getting a response. Weeks of phone tag and rescheduled meetings leave you feeling frustrated. If you've ever worked in sales, I'm sure you've felt this pain.

What happened?

You lost the sale by not controlling the next steps. Before you wrap up a meeting, make sure that you have a commitment on the next step in the process. For example, if you're wrapping up a prospect meeting and the sale hasn't closed, ask your prospect to pull out his calendar to schedule your next meeting date, then agree upon what you will accomplish in that meeting. If your prospect doesn't have his calendar, offer to walk with him back to his office to grab it, or stop by his assistant's desk to book it. At a very minimum, agree on when to call the next day to set the appointment. If you leave with only a vague agreement to meet again, you haven't moved forward.

The second part of this essential sales skill is keeping the ball in your court. The less time there is between your prospect's post-pitch enthusiasm and making the buying decision, the more likely you are to close. For example, let's say you are selling accounting services; you just pitched the CFO only to learn that the CEO is the real decision-maker, so the impressed CFO wraps up by saying he'll discuss it with the CEO and get back with you. What just happened?

You lost control. The ball is not in your court. The last thing you want is someone else making your pitch for you, since that person can't deliver it as strongly or overcome objections like you can.

Instead, stay in the driver's seat. Once the CFO agreed that he was interested in moving forward, you should offer to set up a meeting with him and the CEO to deliver your pitch. You might say, "Since we both have our calendars handy, why don't we call the CEO's assistant to set up that meeting? I'm free the 18th or 20th. Which day works best for you?"

This assumptive closing technique takes the focus off the big question, which is, "Can we call your CEO?" Instead, the focus turns toward asking, "Which day works for you?"

Remember, you're a seller — not a beggar. Don't beg for that next meeting or rely on others to land the meeting for you. Instead, keep control of the ball so you can advance more quickly down the court.

HOW TO DEAL WITH PROSPECT STALL TACTICS

MANY PROSPECTS don't like saying, "no." Other prospects don't feel confident enough to say, "yes." Even though these prospects have different motivations, they both are likely to try to stall the sale, often without sharing strong reasons why they can't move forward. If prospects don't voice outright objections, you can't overcome their concerns.

Many prospects stall by asking for more time, saying, "Give me a call back in 90 days," or, "Let's wait until after an upcoming milestone is behind us. I'll call you then." However, when a prospect tries to stall the sale, make it your first priority to uncover the root reason why he is asking for more time.

First, validate the prospect's hidden objection by saying, "I hear you. This is a big decision, and I want you to be confident." Next, consider this simple open-ended question posed as a statement, which generally garners a pretty candid response: "Tell me more about your hesitation." If you're using a consultative sales approach, remember that your objective is not to manipulate prospects into buying, of course, but to identify the true objection and help each prospect toward a decision that is in his best interest — even if that decision isn't buying from you.

Once the real objection has been unearthed, if you still feel confident what you're offering is in your prospect's best interest, there are several ways you can steer that prospect toward the right decision. For example, if the objection is fear of change, then ask what's at stake. What opportunities would the prospect lose if he just maintained the status quo? If the objection is concern about the time commitment needed for the change, respectfully ask if he anticipates having less to do in the future.

If the prospect is struggling to believe you can deliver on what you've promised, be prepared to prove it. Back up your claims with research, testimonials from clients that will matter to your prospect, relevant referrals that will vouch for your company, or case studies. Even if the prospect discloses that he doesn't have sole decision-making authority, you can still work together to brainstorm approaches to collaboratively sell the idea up the ladder.

If you are simply not able to overcome your prospect's real objection, let him off the hook. Remind him how important it is that your customers are 100 percent certain about moving forward with your company, and that the last thing you want a customer to have is buyer's remorse.

You'll create longer-lasting relationships as a result.

FOLLOW-UP CALLS THAT CLOSE SALES

TOO MANY SALES PROFESSIONALS work tirelessly to land sales meetings, only to lose the sale in the end through a series of poorly executed follow-up calls.

It's easy to mindlessly make follow-up calls checking on the status of a prospect's decision to buy your products or services. Most salespeople typically start out by saying, "I'm just calling to see if you've made a decision to…." Nearly all of us have received an uninspired follow-up call like this before. The message unintentionally delivered is that you need the prospect more than the prospect needs you; you're looking for any business, not just this prospect's business; and you're not terribly motivated to earn that business in the first place.

What constitutes a strong follow-up call? It begins with how well you defined the next step in your last meeting. Never leave a sales meeting without gaining agreement on a firm next step, like a date and time when you'll talk again. Assuming you've done this, you should be calling at a time that has already been set aside by your prospect, eliminating the need to ask for his time, which could open up an opportunity for a stall tactic.

Begin by reminding your prospect of a point of connection, such as a hobby or common acquaintance you share. When you're ready to transition to business, summarize the result of your last meeting. Recap what your prospect liked about your proposal, what objections were posed, and how you resolved those concerns. Explain that not every prospect is a good fit for your company, which should be true, and outline why you believe this partnership is a good fit.

Next, offer a new piece of information to demonstrate your motivation to partner together. It could be some additional research you uncovered that he may find helpful, or an extra added-value element that you want to include in your original project estimate.

Ask your prospect if he has any additional questions, then move to an assumptive close. This might mean, depending upon your sales process, outlining what the first two weeks will look like after executing contracts. You're assuming the prospect has already made the decision to move forward, jumping straight to next steps. You might even suggest meeting the following day to review and sign contracts. Consider narrowing down the timing choices by asking, "Would morning or afternoon tomorrow work better for you?"

If the prospect stalls, don't panic. Just ask follow-up questions until you have a clear understanding of the real objection. Consider saying, "Tell me more about your hesitation to move forward." If you can, sufficiently overcome the objection then attempt to close again.

The key to a good follow-up call is getting it scheduled before leaving the prior meeting, and then planning out a road map for how the next conversation will go. From there, you just need to drive it home.

WHEN HOT PROSPECTS GO COLD

PRETEND THAT A PROSPECT has called, indicating a strong need for what you're selling. You meet with him, identify he is a good fit for your firm, and develop a proposal for how you might work together. You pitch with perfection, see all the right buying signals, and then hear these dreaded words: "Let me get back with you."

However, you're not panicking. After all, the prospect seemed prepared to move forward. You follow up a few days after your meeting, but you don't get a response. Days stretch into weeks, and after several attempts at follow up, you grow increasingly concerned and confused.

Why has this hot prospect gone cold?

Often what happened is the pain that caused your prospect to pick up the phone isn't his biggest problem any longer. Life crept in to divert your prospect's attention. Not to worry. Unless your prospect was a tire kicker, he will likely warm up again. However, there are a few steps you can take to shorten the time between initial interest and ultimate decision. The key is knowing how and when to stay in touch.

In 2011, the National Sales Executive Association reported that 80 percent of sales are made between the 5th and 12th contact with a prospect. This same report indicates that nearly 50 percent of salespeople quit after just the first contact, never making a second contact — and only ten percent make more than three contacts with a prospect. That means that 90 percent of sales teams are working entirely too hard.

You shouldn't interpret lack of a response as a firm "no," but you should get creative. Be smart. Make each of your five or more contacts count. Instead of following up by email or phone like every other salesperson, differentiate yourself in your follow-up methods. Mix it up. Plan a variety of contact points to offer your prospect additional value, making yourself stand out in the process.

Consider a three-dimensional mailing, such as an educational or inspirational book. Consider hiring a courier to deliver that package straight into your prospect's hands for maximum effect.

Another quick, simple strategy is a handwritten note. It's a lost art, but if done well, demonstrates your thoughtfulness. Make sure it doesn't sound like a form letter by commenting on a specific part of your last meeting with the prospect. Keep your message short, and mail it within 24 hours of your last meeting.

Be willing to go the extra mile. Consider inviting your prospect to a special event, or better yet, send a new business lead his way.

After several unreturned contacts, consider calling your prospect before or after hours to ensure you get his voice mail. Script out and practice a voice mail message that explains you are concerned that you're becoming a pest. Ask the prospect directly whether you should stay or go. Explain that you genuinely believe you can solve his problem, but that ultimately, you recognize that it is his choice to make. This strategy helps get you more quickly to a firm response — one way or the other.

Don't assume that the answer is "no" until the prospect says so, but if he does decline, be thankful for the gift of clarity.

GOING, GOING, GONE

WHEN MOST OF US HEAR the phrase "closing techniques," we immediately think of a pushy car salesman frantically trying to sell us a car — any car — before we leave the lot that day. When selling business to business, you often need to use a more delicate approach to closing.

There are dozens of closing techniques, of course, but there are only a few that are effective in business-to-business sales. However, none of these closing techniques are likely to work unless you've established a trusting relationship with your prospect, you've identified a pain point or need that your products or services can address, and your prospect believes you are offering him a good value. The point of all of these strategies is to guide a prospect toward his best decision, and not to manipulate.

With the assumptive-closing technique, you assume your prospect has made the decision to purchase, so your questions focus on future steps. Once you've delivered the quote, you might ask, "Does a Friday delivery meet your needs?" or "Should we schedule the kick-off discussion for Monday?" Even though most salespeople would start out by asking how the quote looks, the assumptive closing technique skips that question altogether — and it works. Behaving confidently, as though the sale has already closed, makes it more difficult for a prospect to stall the sale needlessly.

Conditional closing techniques overcome objections to expedite closing the sale. Conditional closing involves the exchange principle: If you do something for me, I'll exchange the favor. If you are selling technology support services, for example, and your prospect is concerned with the 12-month contract, your conditional close might be something like this: "If I can shorten the contract by three months, are you ready to get started right away?"

The minor points closing technique involves gaining agreement on small points throughout the sales call to get your prospect in the habit of saying yes. With this technique, the key is asking easy questions that don't leave room for a negative response. For example, you might ask, "There are three service options. Which do you like best?" You could also ask, "Do you think this option is important?" Using this approach can be effective with a complex sale, when decision-making may overwhelm your prospect. These small, easy decisions will eventually snowball, simplifying the final decision for your prospects, reducing their anxiety, and most importantly, creating a pattern of saying, "yes."

The opportunity cost closing technique emphasizes the cost of delayed decisions. You might ask, "What is the projected loss in revenue from delaying a decision as little as 30 days?"

Perhaps the most popular closing technique is the straightforward, rational close. This technique works best with prospects that base their decisions on logic, not emotion. First, you will need to remind the prospect of the needs you both identified. Next, recap how your product or service meets those needs. Once your prospect has agreed to both of those summaries, ask if he is ready to move forward.

Identify the closing strategy that is most likely to be effective with your particular prospects, but any closing technique you try needs to feel authentic to you if you're going to knock your next sale out of the park. Regardless, in the end, even if all you do is ask for the business outright, you are likely miles ahead of most of your competitors.

THREE SECRETS TO CLOSING MORE BUSINESS

WHAT IF I TOLD YOU that you're working harder than you should to meet sales targets? If you're not following up with your sales prospects after the initial meeting in the right way, you may be missing a big opportunity that's right under your nose.

Considering how hard salespeople have to work to land a meeting with a prospective customer, it's surprising how little effort is typically put into the follow-up with that prospect after the meeting. The art of a successful follow-up strategy begins while you're meeting with your prospect. Depending on the products or services you're selling, it may be unlikely that anyone could close the sale on the spot — but that just makes it even more important to map out the next step in the process during your initial meeting. If you can agree on the next step right away, you're much more likely to make the sale.

Gain your prospect's firm commitment on a follow-up meeting while you're still in front of him, and clarify the objective for that conversation. Assuming you've already presented your proposal, consider making some strategic assumptions. For example, you might say, "I'm looking forward to our follow-up meeting next Tuesday at 10, where we'll discuss any outstanding questions you may have and finalize our next steps for moving forward." Now that you have the next meeting lined up, there are three simple techniques you should use during that meeting to close more business.

Technique No. 1: Kick off your follow-up meeting by asking great questions and actively listening to what your prospect is telling you. Your primary goal should be to help your prospect make a good decision, not simply to close a sale. That's how you build real relationships and generate a strong referral base. Use open-ended questions and statements to get your prospects to lay their cards on the table. For example, you might say, "Tell me about the elements of the proposal that will have the most impact on your business." You could say, "Tell me about anything that might have been missing or needs to be reworked," or, "Tell me about any other particulars you'd like to be sure are taken into consideration as we move forward."

Technique No. 2: If you have to follow up by phone, ensure you have something new to tell your prospects that adds value for them. No one likes to have a salesperson call simply to "check in." If you've found new information that will help address your prospect's needs, you'll be seen as a partner or consultant, not just a salesperson.

Technique No. 3: If your prospect is unable to make a buying decision in the immediate future, your follow-up strategy should be to stay top-of-mind until the prospect is able to move forward. Be persistent, but not a pest. Mix it up at every touch point. Alternate between calls, email and direct mail, ensuring you are adding value to the relationship each time. Consider asking a current customer to call your prospect, talking about the confidence he has in your company.

Master the art of the successful follow-up to make sure you're maximizing each opportunity, not just eliminating prospects as if there were an unlimited supply.

SECRETS TO EMBRACING REJECTION

WHEN ASKED what contributed most to his NBA career, Michael Jordan said, "I've missed more than 9,000 shots in my career. I've lost almost 300 games. Twenty-six times, I've been trusted to take the game winning shot and missed. I've failed over and over and over again in my life. And that is why I succeed." In fact, according to ESPN, Michael Jordan is number six on the list of basketball players who have missed the most shots in their NBA careers — but no one remembers how many shots you missed. Just like basketball, sales is a numbers game.

Sure, every salesperson prefers to focus on fewer calls that have a higher quality, but no matter your skill and experience, the path to sales success is paved with rejection. Sales guru Dale Carnegie said it best: "Develop success from failures. Discouragement and failure are two of the surest stepping stones to success."

If you're feeling discouraged, there are five strategies you can use to embrace sales rejection, leveraging those rejections to help you reach your targets.

Strategy No. 1: Separate your personal identity from your sales role. Emotionally disconnect from the outcome. When a prospect declines your offer, you have to believe down to your very core that the prospect isn't rejecting you; he is simply rejecting the product or service you're selling. If you take it personally, you may start feeling reluctant to make sales calls, which could cause a dip in your productivity. Remember, selling isn't really about getting someone to say, "yes." It's simply about getting an informed prospect to make a decision.

Strategy No. 2: Disqualifying a prospect is as important as qualifying one. Your time is valuable, so you need to make sure you're spending time with the right prospects. When you are talking with a prospect for the first time, he isn't just evaluating you; you are evaluating whether or not he is a good fit for your company, too. Just because a prospect has dollars to spend doesn't necessarily make him a good client.

Strategy No. 3: Don't put your prospect on a pedestal. Remember that while your prospect may have the money, you have the solution to his problem. Choosing to cultivate this mindset evens the playing field, giving you a clear vision of your prospect as a peer. You are both equals. You may both find it mutually beneficial to partner together — and then again, you may not.

Secret No. 4: Recognize that higher rejection rates lead to more sales and higher earnings. Normalize rejection by setting benchmarks for yourself — how many calls it's going to take you to close a sale. Then, embrace every "no." Each one puts you one step closer to the coveted "yes."

Secret No. 5: When you are staring sales rejection in the face, it's easy to put off picking up the phone for your next call until your mind is right and you're comfortable again. If you wait until you're comfortable, you may never pick up the phone again. You need to be a little uncomfortable to be successful in sales. Be productive, and your attitude will follow your lead. Consistency is the only thing that will help you become more comfortable.

Having a sound sales process and well-differentiated product or service goes a long way, but with sales, half the battle is always in your head. If you can overcome your own barriers as easily as you overcome objections, the market will be yours for the taking.

"SUCCESS IS A LOUSY TEACHER"

MANY PEOPLE throw in the towel after failure, not realizing that failure is actually an inevitable part of innovation. Thomas Edison is reported to have failed more than 1,000 times before finally inventing a practical electric light bulb. He said, "Many of life's failures are people who did not realize how close they were to success when they gave up."

People who are afraid to fail often avoid taking the risks that lead to innovation. They never realize their true potential, because the only way we can improve is through failure. Personally, I can point to a handful of terrible sales calls that led to the fundamental, creative shifts in my sales strategy. Without these shifts, I would never have been as successful as I am today.

Progress cannot coexist with a fear of failure, but you should always aim to fail intelligently. For example, you might test your new ideas on a smaller scale, when possible, to limit your financial risk. Next, recognize failure quickly, assess the cause, adapt and try again. Sales professionals who can let failure lead the way to success are stronger, more confident, and more successful. How can you change your mindset about failure?

Look at failure as a great teacher. Bill Gates said, "Success is a lousy teacher. It seduces smart people into thinking they can't lose." Successful people don't particularly like failure, but they handle it differently than their less successful counterparts. Failure doesn't shatter successful people. Instead, they use it as fuel. They uncover what didn't work, and figure out how to fix the problem. Failure lights their fire.

Dive in headfirst. If you are reluctant to make cold calls, for example, make it the first thing you tackle at the top of every day. Find an accountability partner to make sure you stay the course. Consider setting a seemingly ridiculous objective: Make sure that you fail as miserably as you can at your first three calls of every day until your reluctance is gone. Not only will it demonstrate your ability to survive failure, but you may also learn something new along the way.

Never mistake rejection for failure. Successful salespeople welcome a quick "no," if that "no" is because a prospect genuinely doesn't need their products or services. Quick "no" answers give you more time to focus on qualified, interested prospects.

If you are unsure if you have the risk tolerance to embrace the failure that accompanies innovation, consider the tragic tale of Eastman Kodak. Once a dominant market leader, this company opted to play it safe and focus on its core film business, failing to evolve and capitalize on digital-camera technology. In 2012, the company filed for bankruptcy.

In product development and in sales, sitting still is the same as falling behind.

RESEARCH: OPTIMISTS SELL MORE

OVER THE YEARS, psychologist Martin Seligman has studied the dramatic correlation between a salesperson's personal outlook and his ability to close sales. According to Entrepreneur.com and these studies, optimists do indeed sell more than pessimists — 33 percent more, in fact. They seem to handle rejection more easily, and often, rejection just increases their persistence. They are more likely to stay motivated on their own, and less likely to give up when a sales call doesn't go well.

However, optimism in this context doesn't mean having an unrealistically positive outlook all the time. Instead, it's all about how a person deals with setbacks.

Not a "glass is half full" person? Don't despair. This same study confirms that a pessimist can be coached into having more optimistic traits, at least when it comes to his outlook on sales.

Optomists see the cause of a customer saying "no" to purchase as external to them — a customer's choice to a specific situation and not a universal issue or trend. On the other hand, pessimists take each rejection more personally, assuming that it is a recurring issue they will always face.

If you are a sales pessimist, take these steps, based on Seligman's research, to alter your selling vantage point. It's called the ABCDE model.

Be on the lookout for elements of sales adversity (A), your related beliefs (B) and the consequences (C) of those beliefs. If you made 20 sales calls today and weren't able to make it past a single gatekeeper, that is your adversity. Your belief may be that future calls are in vain. The consequence of that belief is that you just go through the motions on future calls without giving it much effort, and your fears become reality.

To overcome that internal negative talk, dispute (D) it, offering alternative reasons for the lack of sales success and questioning the usefulness of the pessimism. Actively tell yourself, for example, that you're new in your role or calling on a new type of client. With time and persistence, your skills will improve, and you will successfully reach more prospects. Tomorrow will be a better day.

Finally, pay attention and celebrate how arguing against self-defeating talk energizes (E) you. It's okay to admit that you are still a little disappointed or frustrated, but acknowledge that you're not letting it get you down because things will improve.

For a significant behavior change to stick, it is vital to involve others for support and accountability. Find a mentor or supportive peer to share in your struggles and victories — but make sure you're choosing your friends wisely. Late motivational speaker and author Jim Rohn said, "You are the average of the five people you spend the most time with." Do others share your newfound optimism? Fire catches.

CHANGES IN BUYER BEHAVIOR CRITICAL TO BUSINESS SURVIVAL

A SIGNIFICANT SHIFT in buyer behavior has occurred over the last several years, one that has not only changed the very essence of the role of a salesperson, but how we market to consumers as well. The origin of this shift is three-fold: the Internet now plays a stronger role in informing buyers about products and services, a new paradigm in group decision-making has developed, and there is now an increasing expectation for a heightened buying "experience."

Our 24/7 access to the Internet and our growing reliance upon it as our primary source of new product information have caused a significant change in buyer behavior. Because buyers no longer rely on salespeople for basic product information, the role of the sales professional has changed dramatically. Once thought of as subject-matter experts, in many business categories, salespeople have been relegated to the role of order-taker, if only because consumers come to the table armed with information without ever engaging a member of the sales team. For salespeople to stay relevant, they have to offer customers more specialized support.

To further complicate matters, a large percentage of consumers now turn to social media networks for product and service input from their friends and acquaintances before visiting company websites or conducting a Google search. We can no longer assume that buyers make decisions in isolation. The old model of one salesperson overcoming the objections of a single buyer rarely holds true these days. Now, we have to look at most buyers as being part of a network where collaborative decisions are made. The key is figuring out where your buyers spend their time online, so that you can play an active part in their conversations.

Once a short list of top providers has been collected, consumers have high expectations for their first contact with the sales team. Today's consumers value the overall buying "experience" as much as they value the features and benefits of the product or service itself.

Because of this expectation, sellers have to figure out how to humanize the buying experience, creating a real connection with prospective buyers right out of the gate. The difference between competing products and services has become so narrow that your customers' buying experiences could be your best opportunity to stand out in the marketplace.

The implications of these three shifts in buyer behaviors are enormous for business owners and marketers. They shake the very foundation of the sales process we've always known — but in the end, we need to adapt, or else we will face the harsh reality of lost market share.

HOW SALES TEAMS CAN WORK THEMSELVES OUT OF A JOB

THE INFORMATION AGE is pushing many industries down the path of commoditization, where consumers don't see much of a difference between you and your competitors, so their purchasing decisions become overly focused on price. This is a dangerous position for any company.

This shift is due in large part to the depth of information available to prospects before a salesperson is even engaged, which has forever changed the role sales professionals play in closing a sale. Long gone are the days where sharing features and benefits is enough. Sales professionals must take on a more strategic role to maintain relevance, differentiate their brands, and add value to the sales process, shifting consumer decisions away from the price tag.

Real, tangible value must be created to break through the barriers of commoditization, and it isn't built on clichés like "great customer service." Your differentiator must be significant and important to your customers. It might be a product or service differentiator, or it could very well be the unique, strategic insight offered by your sales team.

A recent Huthwaite study uncovered an unexpected consumer behavior, shedding light onto how sales professionals can create value. Thousands of customers reported being faced with several competitor choices with no strong differentiators. Interestingly, customers did not select the low-cost offering in most instances.

Skilled sales professionals offered insights that those buyers couldn't see on their own, which is challenging given the depth of information a prospect can find online about a company before ever setting foot in the door.

You have to convince prospects that you are strategically important and that other competitors are poor substitutes. What is your sales team doing to convince customers you are a vital strategic partner, one that is difficult to find in a crowded marketplace? If your sales team can't clearly explain what makes your company different, you're encouraging customers to focus more closely on prices, which could ultimately cause lower margins and make it difficult to cost-justify a skilled sales force. In short: many salespeople may be working themselves out of a job.

Start solving this problem by asking the right questions. Customers place more value on what they have to say than anything you could tell them. With any new prospect, you must conduct a thorough needs assessment, asking high-impact questions that will help the prospect fully realize his needs. He may even find one that he hasn't recognized before.

Next, position yourself as an indispensable strategic partner by identifying an unanticipated solution for the buyer's problem or revealing an unexpected opportunity the buyer didn't know about. You could also establish yourself as a solutions broker, serving as a broader resource. Consider partnering with a non-competing vendor to offer your prospect a broader "soup to nuts" solution to his problem.

When your objective is to create customized value, no two sales will look alike. While this strategy requires more effort, you are more likely to generate higher margins, building long-term relationships with customers who aren't just price shopping.

PRE-SELLING TO CONNECTED BUYERS

OVER THE LAST DECADE, the buying experience has been completely reinvented, and companies that have been slow to adapt are quickly losing revenue and market share.

A 2011 Sales Executive Council study showed that 57 percent of the buying process is completed before a prospect even makes contact with a sales professional. We now live in a world of connected buyers, whose minds are almost completely made up before they choose to interact with a member of your sales team. Most of the information they want to know is already at their fingertips, day and night.

That's why it is vital that your brand engage in pre-selling — influencing buyer decisions before they ever make contact with your brand.

Start by identifying why connected buyers begin exploring the types of products and services you have to offer. Although these reasons will vary by industry, some common reasons for change are a growing sense of dissatisfaction with a competing vendor, an advertising campaign, or a change in circumstances — like an expansion into a new location, a significant new competitor coming to market, or an influx of venture capital opening up their pocketbooks. If you can figure out what triggers buyers to reach out to you, you can make sure your name is in the right place at the right time.

When connected buyers enter the exploration phase, their top resources are the Internet, their friends and the community. Because much of a buyer's decision is made before you're directly involved, make sure that your website performs well in common keyword searches, that it's customized for usage on any type of handheld device, and that the information your typical buyer wants is easy to find.

Work to ensure your connected buyers are receiving positive third-party feedback about your company by controlling what you can — allowing top influencers in the market to try your offering at a discount, or for free, to create brand champions. You should also maintain a strong social-media presence, encourage your happy customers to write testimonials on top review sites, and include those testimonials on your website.

Follow these guidelines to ensure your company is among those being considered by the connected buyer. When potential buyers do make contact, know that most won't distinguish between a customer-service representative and sales professional. Both teams must be armed with advanced sales skills to effectively engage today's new evolution of buyer.

NAVIGATING FIRST CONTACT WITH CONNECTED BUYERS

THE INTERNET HAS CREATED a marketplace built predominantly of connected buyers who make decisions before they ever make contact with a sales professional. Because information about your company and competitors is readily available online, sales support is often unnecessary early in the buying process. Has your sales strategy evolved to fit this new reality, or are you facing market extinction?

Early in your first meeting with connected buyers, focus on determining what information they've gathered so far and how they got to you. Needs assessment and product education will follow, but only after finding out what they already know. After all, connected buyers are not interested in starting from scratch; you must join them where they already are in the buying process. By understanding the steps they've taken before reaching you, their reason for deciding to actually make a call, and what they expect from the sales process, you will be able to guide the conversation in a way that's comfortable for your connected buyers.

Start by asking your connected buyers how they learned about your company. Thank them for considering your company, showing appreciation for their business and positively reinforcing their decision to continue exploring your company. Reiterate the one-sentence elevator pitch that this connected buyer has already seen on your website, and then ask what triggered the decision to seek out more information about your products or services. With the right follow-up questions, you'll uncover the factors that are most important to closing the sale.

Next, ask how long this connected buyer has been exploring different options, and follow up with questions about the exploration process. For example, you will want to know who was involved, what steps were taken, what put your company on the short list, and the decision-making timeline in order to uncover the critical buying information you'll need to advance the sale.

Finally, recap for the prospective buyer what you've learned about his needs. If he agrees, explain your value proposition. Based on what you've learned about the buyer so far, tailor your pitch on the spot.

If a one-call close isn't likely in your business, ask for a follow-up meeting to discuss the prospective buyer's needs in greater depth. Be sure to confirm which key stakeholders will be present, names you should already know from your earlier questions.

To stay relevant to connected buyers, learn how to change your approach. Altering your line of questioning, based on what you're hearing from your prospects, will help you personalize your pitch in a meaningful way that's sure to resonate with your connected buyers.

PERILS OF UNINTENTIONAL SALESPEOPLE

EVEN IF YOU ARE AN OWNER or manager, to some degree, you're still in sales — intentionally or not.

Unintentional salespeople don't think of sales as their primary role, but they find themselves spending much of their day doing just that — from selling their expertise to selling ideas or products. Think about the entrepreneur who is selling his ideas to financial backers. Consider the business owner or manager who sells his services in virtually every personal and professional conversation, simply due to his belief in what he offers. How about those in professional service roles — like attorneys and doctors — who desire to grow their practices, but may prefer not to entrust their sales efforts to others?

Although they mean well, unintentional salespeople often have little formal sales training and may struggle with these four common challenges. If you can avoid these pitfalls, you're guaranteed to improve your sales performance.

Self-Defeating Talk: If you have been known to say, "I'm not a salesperson," consider taking a different perspective, without the self-defeating talk. Over 90 percent of professional positions have some kind of sales component, since sales is simply the art of persuading others to consider your solution. Take pride in your ability to sell.

Over-Zealous Delivery: Owners are often guilty of delivering a sales pitch with an abundance of enthusiasm. While passion can be powerful in sales, it can also cause someone to talk too fast, overwhelming a prospect with too much information, without listening closely. Passion can also make it difficult to know when to stop talking and close the sale.

Racing Past the Fork: In many cases, it's appropriate to prepare a formal presentation for a sales pitch. When you do, and your prospect interrupts with questions, what do you do? Do you respond to his questions, and then too quickly veer back to the presentation? Unintentional salespeople often do this. Instead, think about your presentation as simply a method for telling your story in a way that's designed to encourage interruptions. The next time a prospect asks you a question, welcome that two-way interaction. It's an opportunity to build trust.

Avoiding the Post-Mortem: A post-mortem is an analysis of what worked and what didn't work during a sales meeting. Avoid moving ahead to the next opportunity until you've stepped back to uncover any weaknesses in the pitch you just delivered. The post-mortem is critical for continuous improvement so you can prevent repeat mistakes. Think about what language resonated most with the prospect, what fell flat, what you would continue doing, and what you would modify if you had a second chance.

If you're able to leap past these four selling obstacles, you will be well on your way to becoming the intentional salesperson you never thought you could be.

THE ART OF SELLING PROFESSIONAL SERVICES

PROFESSIONAL SERVICE FIRMS include law firms, accounting practices, insurance agencies, architectural firms and financial services companies. Old business development strategies — like relying solely on repeat business and passive referrals — have been turned completely upside-down in these fields. The old ways of growing business no longer result in sustainable growth for most firms, and competitive pressure is mounting.

However, "sales" is still a dirty word among many professional service companies. These professionals don't want to admit that selling is a part of their job. Networking means attending social events without necessarily telling people about their firms.

Now many of these practices with this mindset are struggling to survive, let alone grow.

Firms that are growing are adapting to the changing marketplace by applying a few basic tenets that anyone can use.

First, you have to get over the stigma of sales. If you're not comfortable selling, ask yourself these questions. Do you believe you are truly helping to improve your clients' lives or the performance of their companies? Are you helping to take away their pain? If so, you're doing prospects a disservice by not trying to help them.

Create a consistent process. Just responding to inbound requests doesn't position you to get the business you actually want and deserve. Get in the driver's seat. Learn how many calls you need to make per week or month to grow your business. Systemize your calling efforts so others can easily replicate your successes.

Share your passion about what you are selling. Today's buyer is looking for a service provider with conviction, someone who can help him make smarter decisions, not just a yes-man looking to close a deal. Speak up, and be an agent of change. This will set you apart, and most prospects will respect you for it.

Understand the nuances of trust-based selling. In the world of professional service sales, you are the product. There is a point in the decision-making process when prospects are assessing your trustworthiness. You can earn trust by demonstrating genuine concern for both the prospect and his company, and listening more than you're talking. This is another reason why shooting straight is essential. If your prospect appreciates your candor, it builds trust, and the sale will likely close. If the prospect doesn't respect your honesty, it probably wasn't a good fit anyway.

You must make the prospect understand the intangible. Selling a service can be challenging. Even without a product to hold, you have to help your prospects see the value of what you're offering. You can share case studies about customers who faced similar challenges or provide industry best practices to demonstrate that your education and training can be of benefit. Lastly, let your prospect witness what a typical day is like inside your company, to help him understand what it means to work with your firm.

If waiting for the phone to ring is no longer an effective selling strategy, it's time to get yourself out of the office. Build your prospect list, prepare for your calls, and start making appointments. After all, you have some really good news to share.

CULTIVATING RELATIONSHIPS WITH DISTINCT BUYER TYPES

IN TODAY'S INCREASINGLY competitive world, it's vital to know your audience and what language resonates with it the most. Savvy sales professionals are able to identify a buyer's preferences within minutes, predicting what will influence his decision to buy. If you can access this powerful information, you can tailor your pitch accordingly and close more sales.

There are five distinct buyer "types" — the financial buyer, the technical buyer, the user buyer and the executive buyer, and if you're lucky, you'll also meet the champion buyer as well.

The financial buyer is most concerned about price, since he is typically in control of the budget. Often, he is also the final decision maker. At times, he may be willing to sacrifice quality to get a good deal. This buyer often asks about the return on his investment, so be prepared to answer questions about ROI.

The technical buyer usually influences the purchasing decision, but he generally doesn't make the final call. Instead, the real decision maker asks him to find options and make recommendations. Due to his unique perspective, he may have his own objectives, which differ from the decision maker's. The technical buyer wants to ensure that what you're offering is the correct technical solution, and that it won't cause him added headaches.

The user buyer is likely the one who will actually use your product in his daily routine, and his primary interest is how your product or service will help him do his job. User buyers often ask about technical support, or request to speak to other users about their experiences.

The executive buyer often has the final say. First and foremost, he is interested in how your offering will help the company advance its strategic goals, generate more profit, grow sales or drive more customers. Executive buyers will ask how your product or service will help them compete in the marketplace more effectively.

Occasionally, one of these four buyer types may transition into the role of champion that is so impressed by your product or service that he begins to advocate on your behalf within the company. You may sway an already supportive buyer into a champion by simply explaining that you need his help. Champions may request your help to overcome internal obstacles. Often, they will provide insight into key issues, schedules and the competition.

More often than not, multiple buyer types will be involved with complex or expensive purchases. Identify each type of buyer, and then adjust your sales pitch to ensure its relevant and compelling for each particular audience.

UNDERSTAND PROSPECTS' PERSONALITIES

STRONG SALESPEOPLE read their prospects quickly and adapt accordingly. Prospects can generally be categorized as having one of four personality types: the analytical prospect, the driver, the amiable prospect and the expressive prospect. Once you've determined your prospect's personality type, you can adapt your approach to help build a solid relationship. After all, birds of a feather flock together.

Analytical prospects are thinkers. They are dependable, organized and have an appreciation for detail. They can come across as standoffish until you get to know them. As a sales professional, your best approach with this prospect is just to get down to business. Analytical prospects aren't there to make friends, and they will appreciate an efficient meeting. Ask questions to better appreciate their business challenges. Be thorough and precise when you are explaining your products or services.

Amiable prospects are good listeners. They are friendly, approachable and focused on building relationships. They are more sensitive than other prospect personality types. They struggle to make quick decisions, and they often waver after the decision is made. If you're selling to amiable prospects, start by building trust. They will make a decision to buy based primarily on their comfort level with you. Use a soft, comforting tone when conversing. Help them feel good about the decision to work with you. Even after the contract is signed, they may continue to need reassurance about their decision.

Prospects known as drivers like to take action and are quick to do so. They are also likely to stand by their decisions. However, they aren't likely to be great listeners. They may not appreciate anything that interferes with their ability to act on their agenda. They can be inflexible and impatient when things don't go according to plan. If you can demonstrate your appreciation for a driver's time, you will be rewarded. Script your presentation in advance. Cut it down to a few impactful minutes. If drivers want additional details, they will ask questions. Give them enough information to make a decision, and then close the deal.

Expressive prospects like to talk. They love the art of conversation, and they love a good audience even more. They have a tendency to digress, and they are easily bored. They bring up their positive and negative reactions quickly, often without much forethought. They would rather agree with you than argue, even when they see the issue differently. If you're selling to expressive prospects, use their names often to make them feel special. Keep the discussion light. Be comfortable chitchatting, but you also need to be ready to lead them back to the point.

While every prospect is a little analytical and amiable, driving at some times and expressive at others, one of the four personality types is usually dominant. The more quickly you can discern your prospect's type, the more likely you are to connect and close the sale.

ARM YOUR SALES TEAM WITH BUYER PERSONAS

GREAT METHOD ACTORS engage in an extensive process to get inside the heads of their characters, truly understanding their personas, and because of this process, they consistently deliver stellar performances. Similarly, if your sales force had deep understanding of its potential buyers, not only would this improve its ability to connect in a more meaningful way, this would also allow it to tailor its pitch to make sure qualified prospects become buyers.

Understanding your ideal prospect's persona is like building a fictional version of the prospect, based on real data about your best prospects and customers — like demographics, behavior patterns, buying patterns, decision-making processes, or even life goals.

Make sure your ideal buyer persona is objective. Don't base this persona on your own gut impulses; do the necessary research. Start by identifying a dozen ideal customers and a dozen ideal prospects that are likely to spend 15 to 20 minutes talking with you. If you're in a referral-based business, consider talking to a few influencers as well. Even though incentives may not be necessary, you might consider offering them gift cards to thank them for their time. Call them to schedule a phone interview, making it clear you're not trying to sell them anything.

Be thoughtful about which questions you ask. For example, you might ask: What is your title? Who do you report to, and what are the titles of those who report to you? What goes on during your typical day? What's the size of your company? How old are you, how many children do you have, and are you married? What do you do outside of work? What organizations do you belong to? What's challenging about your job or life? What do you value most at work? What are your common concerns when a company in our category approaches you?

Once you've gathered this data, look for as many similarities as possible. Next, create a story line for that customer that will be easy for your salespeople to remember. For example, your primary buyer may be a family man with two kids and a golden retriever. He tries to work in a game of golf every few weeks, but it's tough with all of the kids' activities. He appreciates candor and hard work in those around him. He makes buying decisions based on trust and relationships, only later comparing features, benefits and pricing. He has big career aspirations, so a solution that will allow him to advance his career will be given serious consideration.

While your customer persona may not fit every ideal customer exactly, it can accurately represent the needs of a larger group. Understanding your buyers' motivations, expectations and goals can help your team deliver a more tailored sales experience, inevitably closing more sales.

BUYING SIGNALS HELP AVOID OVERSELLING

SALES PROFESSIONALS have two ears and one mouth for a reason. The formula for sales success is 80 percent listening and only 20 percent talking. Good listeners "hear" more than just the words their prospects speak. They also pick up on nonverbal cues.

Interested prospects inevitably communicate buying signals once they make the decision to do business with you. That decision is typically made first from a place of emotion. Once that emotional commitment is made, the prospect begins to seek rational justification for the decision, which is when buying signals emerge.

If you're not tuned in to these buying signals, you may make the fatal mistake of overselling by continuing your sales pitch past the point when your prospect is ready for you to close the sale. Not only are you providing your prospect with superfluous material that could raise further objections that aren't already on the table, but talking too much is also an indication of insecurity and weakness. Overselling can quickly cause the death of a sale.

Some of the most common buying signals include: smiling and nodding, a sudden leaning forward in the seat, reading the fine print, working through related calculations, suggesting you review the proposal with another person on the team or asking questions related to closing the sale. Closing questions are often about pricing, financing, payment terms, production details and delivery logistics.

While it may seem counterintuitive that objections could be buying signals, when prospects object to your price, they are really admitting that they're interested in working with you, provided you can help them get comfortable with your price tag. They are seeking rational justification to support the emotional decision that has already been made. Help them get there by restating your value proposition's relationship to your price.

Savvy sales professionals pick up on subtle cues by watching for behavior and body language changes that differ from the prospect's previous behavior, indicating purchase intent. It can be as though a switch were flipped.

If the prospect didn't look through the product samples in the first part of your meeting but all the sudden begins browsing your materials with a renewed interest, he may have decided to move forward and is simply seeking more details regarding how he might do that.

Most often, when a prospect holds his chin, he's giving serious thought to your proposition. If there's a natural break in the conversation, allow the prospect time to think by avoiding the inclination to fill up the silence. If your prospect looks up and makes eye contact with you, the decision to proceed has likely been made, and it's time for your closing question.

To avoid overselling, just open your eyes and ears. All the answers are right there in front of you.

DECODING PROSPECTS' SECRET LANGUAGE

LET'S FACE IT. Prospects have a language of their own. Sometimes they say one thing when they really mean another. Shocking, right? The language differences between sellers and buyers are akin to those between men and women; they're often worlds apart. Fortunately, prospects have a few common responses that, once decoded, will help even the playing field.

Prospect Code: "I'm happy with our current provider."

Common Translation: "You haven't piqued my interest enough to get me to consider shifting from my comfortable surroundings to unknown territory."

Prospect Code: "It's not in the budget."

Common Translation: "I could afford it if there were a return on my investment, but you just haven't demonstrated enough value to justify the price."

Prospect Code: "Send me more information."

Common Translation: "I'm stalling. I don't really see the value in what you're proposing yet, but I just don't have the courage to tell you."

Prospect Code: "I need to talk it over with someone else."

Common Translation: "I don't have the authority to make this decision on my own," or more commonly, "I'm just stalling because I'm not quite sold on your products or services, and I'm using someone else as the scapegoat."

Prospect Code: "Call me back in a few months."

Common Translation: "I'm going to tell you to call me back, but I intend to screen you like bugs in the summer. Don't count on reaching me anytime soon!"

Prospect Code: "I need to think it over."

Common Translation: "I'm still a bit uneasy and want to get some reinforcement from my inner circle before I agree."

Prospect Code: "I'll have to look at the numbers."

Common Translation: "I might be interested, but I have to think about how to negotiate a better deal (or work it into my budget) before we can move forward."

Prospect Code: "That's a long commitment."

Common Translation: "I don't know you well enough to trust you just yet. Let's date before we get married."

When prospects speak in code, they're often stalling. It means they aren't quite ready to share their real objections — likely because they don't want to hurt your feelings, are embarrassed or are anxious about telling you the truth.

While these translations don't hold true 100 percent of the time, more often than not, they are accurate. To determine the true meaning of an objection, hold your ground and dig a bit more deeply with your prospect to reach the real root.

THE SILENT SALES KILLER – BODY LANGUAGE

SEVENTY TO NINETY PERCENT of what we communicate is shared through body language, not words. If you're in a sales role, your ability to interpret and react quickly to body language cues from prospects will either make you or break you. More often than not, the reason a sales pitch fails is never vocalized. However, body language can give away an objection before the prospects are ready to voice their concerns. If you're going to be a savvy communicator, you need to be able to interpret the subtle meaning behind your prospect's body language.

In reading a prospect's body language, look for gestures like:

Touching the Face: When a prospect touches his face with his index finger pointing up and another finger covering his mouth, creating an "L" shape, he may be disagreeing with you.

Covering the Mouth: A finger covering the mouth might be a prospect's subconscious attempt to withhold something. If you see this gesture after he's voiced an objection, ask probing questions to find out if there's another objection still lingering.

Arms Folded: Folded arms could mean your prospect is hiding something. It could also mean that he doesn't like what he is hearing. Overcome negative body language by giving the person something to hold, like a brochure. Occupying his hands can help open a prospect up.

Clenched Hands: Two clenched hands supporting one's head can mean your prospect is frustrated or impatient. Clenched hands on a desk are easier to overcome. Regardless, these gestures telegraph a negative response before it's vocalized. Try another strategy before that negative response becomes official.

Hand Supporting the Head: A hand supporting the head could signal boredom. Finger or foot tapping can show boredom, too. Inject more energy and inter-activity into your pitch.

Stroking the Chin: This means your prospect is assessing what you're sharing with him.

Open Palms: This says your prospect is open to what you have to say, or he's already formed an allegiance with you. Direct eye contact and a tilted head also indicate interest.

Relaxed Brows: Relaxed brows indicate ease in the conversation. A tense brow line may indicate tension or confusion.

Smiling Eyes: It's hard to fake a natural smile. Smile lines around the eyes mean it is probably genuine.

As a student of body language, don't let a single gesture derail your pitch. Sometimes a tapping foot is just a sign of too much coffee. It is not an exact science, so be sure not to overreact at every movement. However, if you see your prospect starting to mirror your gestures, you know you're on the right path. After you've made your pitch, if your prospect leans forward with unclasped hands and smiles, it's time to close.

BOOST SALES BY TALKING THEIR TALK

LINGUISTICS IS THE STUDY of human language. Since a sales pitch is essentially just a conversation between two people, those with a deep understanding of the nuances behind the spoken word will be more successful sales professionals.

One of the most crucial sales-linguistic skills is monitoring your prospect's intonation. A few minutes into a sales meeting, when a prospect gets comfortable with you and relaxes, you should hear the prospect's baseline intonation — his natural pitch, volume and cadence.

Pay attention to changes in a prospect's baseline intonation. Changes might indicate boredom, excitement or anxiety. If he begins talking louder or faster, it could mean he isn't being completely truthful with you or is holding something back. Similarly, if his body language alters significantly, something is changing for your prospect internally. Great salespeople can identify this change and adapt before prospects talk themselves out of a sale.

For years, salespeople have been taught to use a strategy called "mirroring and matching," where you subtly align your body language with that of your prospect. This can build rapport with a prospect, since they will feel connected with you. The same principles hold true when it comes to language and speech.

People process information using their sensory systems — taste, smell, touch, hearing and sight. This knowledge can play an important role in your sales conversation. For example, you will know your prospect is relying on sight if a prospect says, "I really like the way this looks." Savvy sales professionals who recognize this might reply, "I often hear from our customers how delighted they are with the sleek design of our products." By doing this, you're validating the sensory mode the prospect is using to make a decision about buying from you.

Make claims about your products or services without inviting your prospect to disagree by simply adjusting the way you phrase your statement. For example, if you run a medical practice and you're trying to ask other physicians to refer more patients your way, you wouldn't want to claim that you offer the best care in the city within your specialty, since that invites questions.

Instead, you might explain that after referring patients to your practice, other physicians have received highly positive feedback from their patients. Better yet, tell them about a recent marketplace survey you've conducted citing that 95 percent of doctors who have referred to your practice report extremely high levels of satisfaction. Prospective buyers or influencers are unlikely to argue with what other people think, especially when those people aren't around to argue back.

Learning how to talk the talk in sales will help you deliver deeper prospect engagement and more closed sales.

TIPS FOR SELLING TO FIRST-TIME BUYERS

SAVVY SALES PROFESSIONALS adjust their approach when selling to first-time buyers, especially when their products or business services are complex. If you approach first-time buyers and seasoned buyers the same way, you could end up with a very unhappy customer.

To identify a prospect's foundation of understanding, ask early in your discovery process if the prospect has ever worked with a firm like yours. If he hasn't worked with a similar firm before, explain the steps in the buying process, how to effectively compare your firm to competitors, or costs that should be taken into account. Build long-term loyalty by arming your prospect with the information he needs to make an informed decision that is in his best interest.

Next, ask your prospect how he would define success in a partnership with your firm. This question will help you determine if the prospect's expectations for the partnership are realistic. If they aren't, this is an opportunity for a candid conversation about expectations that benefits both parties. It's important to have this kind of conversation sooner, rather than later.

Go on to outline what's essential for a successful relationship. If you're selling a business service that requires your prospect to make substantial changes, be transparent about what's required. Share success stories about clients who have embraced change, and possibly describe failure that occurred because a client resisted change. Your prospects will appreciate your honesty, and their reactions will indicate whether or not they'll be a good fit for your company. Real sales professionals only want to work with customers if it's a mutually beneficial relationship that leads them to buy again and even refer your products or services to others.

If you're working with new buyers, you need to focus more intently on building trust. Build trust by asking questions, listening more than talking, and by making it clear you genuinely care about what your prospect is saying. Don't push too hard. Give them a reason to trust you by sharing evidence of successful client partnerships. Share a specific story about a past client, the challenges he faced, the strategy you implemented to help him rise to those challenges, and the specific results the strategy generated.

Unfortunately, many new buyers aren't able to foresee the inevitable bumps in the road that might come up along the way. Make sure your new buyers can anticipate curveballs. This will help you build trust with them, while also making sure their enthusiasm doesn't slowly diminish.

As you walk first-time buyers through the sales process, be patient, build trust, outline expectations, and warn them about possible obstacles. Remember this initial time investment is a necessary part of creating long-term loyalty.

PERSUADING CEOS TO BUY

CEO-LEVEL SALES CALLS can be intimidating. They certainly aren't for the faint of heart, but with great risks come great rewards.

Starting at the top certainly has its benefits, since CEOs are typically the ultimate decision makers. However, you need to be sure that what you're selling fulfills a need that's already on the CEO's radar, not a product that someone down the line would normally handle. You cannot afford to burn a bridge with a CEO, and wasting time is a fast path to disaster.

There are a handful of tried and true strategies for reaching a CEO. Many try to climb the corporate ladder by making contact at a lower level first, and then selling their way up. While that first contact may be more easily achieved using this method, the path upward can be a long one.

Others ask a mutual connection to introduce them to the CEO. You might also try attending events you believe the CEO will attend in the hopes of a seemingly accidental meeting. Last, but not least, you can simply cold call.

Most sales professionals have better luck reaching CEOs very early or late in the day. When you do reach the CEO, avoid the traditional question-based sales approach momentarily, and focus on quickly piquing his curiosity in order to earn a meeting.

If you're unable to reach the CEO directly, take a straightforward approach with his assistant by simply telling your story. Offer to send a short email explaining why you're calling, and why it's important you speak with the CEO. If the executive assistant sees value in what you're offering, your message will likely reach the CEO's hands.

Once you finally land the coveted meeting with a CEO, it's time to get your game face on. This isn't your average sales pitch.

What CEOs crave most is to have interesting conversations with smart people who can help them better understand the problems they face and explain how to solve them. What they dread most is a formal, rehearsed sales pitch that focuses on demonstrating knowledge more than facilitating an actual conversation.

To have credibility with a CEO, you can't approach the meeting just as a vendor. You have to be seen as a peer who can solve problems by talking on his level.

Identify through questioning the challenges the CEO faces and share real examples, with limited detail, of how you've helped other CEOs overcome those same challenges. Address some of the risks the CEO will face if he chooses to work with you, but always focus on the future, since the CEO may be one of the only people within an organization with a long-term vision.

Wrap up by summarizing the next steps for generating results within the CEO's organization, not simply by explaining the next steps in the sales process. A typical CEO thinks on his feet, so don't be hesitant to ask about his decision in the moment if body language indicates one has been made.

CASTING YOUR NET FOR SUCCESS

THERE ARE NUMEROUS WAYS to gather leads for your sales team. Many companies try advertising, website marketing and telemarketing, for example. However, when you're selling to other businesses, networking can be one of the most effective tools of all.

Networking lets you find people you might not have met through cold calling, and it also helps you develop relationships with prospects before you make a sales call, which makes those prospects more receptive to a meeting.

If it's so effective, why does networking cause anxiety in so many people? Some people are afraid of rejection, and others don't want to be perceived as boring or pushy. It's useful to consider Zig Ziglar's acronym for FEAR — False Evidence Appearing Real. We convince ourselves networking should be feared, when in reality, that fear is unfounded.

If you fear networking, think about it this way: Your sole purpose is to connect with people and learn something about them. All you need is the prospect's business card and a point of connection so that you can follow up productively. Simply ask questions and be authentically engaged in the conversation. Let the other person remember how easy you were to talk to.

Now, doesn't that take the pressure off? You're not there to close a sale. If you build rapport with someone, he will ask about your background — and when you ask for his card, he will likely ask for yours. It's an understated networking strategy, which can set reluctant networkers at ease.

Here are a few additional tips for getting the most from your networking activities — casting your "net" for sales success.

Check out the territory. Before a networking event, ask organizers for a list of attendees. Identify prospects you want to meet beforehand by checking them out on Facebook and LinkedIn, identifying what you may have in common.

Set a goal, like the specific number of prospects you want to meet.

Find at least one point of connection with each person with whom you speak. Make notes about something significant your prospect said. This could include hobbies, common acquaintances or personal causes. Use these as icebreakers when you follow up.

Relax. You're not there to close a sale; your objective is simply to learn more about other people. About 95 percent of communication is non-verbal, so make sure you're projecting confidence. Don't cross your arms or take other defensive postures. Smiling will help you relax, and it will put the other person at ease.

Focus on the other person. Learn what is important to him. Find out what keeps him up at night, and help him solve that problem. Don't just promote your services.

Show interest and enthusiasm. People love feeling interesting. Listen and ask thoughtful questions. Your goal is just to engage prospects in conversation, building rapport.

The best way to start a relationship is to be helpful. Ask the prospect what his ideal client looks like, and provide a possible lead. Maybe he will do the same for you.

Don't let the trail go cold after the networking event. Stay in touch with people, even if they aren't ideal prospects right now. You never know when you might need that connection.

MAKE MEMORABLE IMPRESSIONS AT NETWORKING EVENTS

DO YOU FIND YOURSELF attending countless networking events without generating much new business? It's possible you're not leaving a memorable impression.

Don't take it personally. Most networking group participants focus on what they're going to say next, not what other people have to say. Deploying attention-grabbing strategies can be essential to generating a real return on your time investment in networking.

Start by wearing your nametag in a place where people aren't afraid to look at it, slightly beneath your shoulder. Better yet, avoid paper nametags that inevitably curl or fall off, and invest in a more permanent nametag. Make sure your name and your company's name are printed in large, easy-to-read letters.

Make sure you're one of the best-dressed people in the room. You only have three seconds to make a strong first impression, and once that impression has been made, it's nearly irreversible. People appraise your visual and behavioral appearance from head to toe. They observe your demeanor, mannerisms and body language — and even assess your grooming and accessories, like your watch, portfolio and handbag. If your outward appearance suggests success and professionalism, others will remember you as a valuable contact.

When introducing yourself, say your first name, pause, and then say your full name. Repetition improves the chance your name sticks to memory. For example, say, "I'm Angela. Angela Anderson."

Develop a memorable greeting. If you're a loan officer, say, "I help make the dreams of business owners come true by connecting them with start-up capital." If you own a record shop, consider saying, "Hi, I'm Rick. Rick Henley. I believe in second chances for people and vinyl. That's why I sell pre-owned records at my shop over in Midtown."

If you're shy, bring a wingman. For example, you could bring a colleague who knows you well. You could approach new people together by introducing and bragging on one another. "This is Jenny. She's a financial planning whiz. I wouldn't trust my money with anyone else!"

Fully engage in each conversation. Don't focus on who's entering the room or what you're going to say next. Maintain eye contact, smile, ask thoughtful follow-up questions and sincerely compliment people. The late author and poet Maya Angelou once famously said, "I've learned that people will forget what you said; people will forget what you did; but people will never forget how you made them feel."

Use storytelling to engage everyone you speak with. Have a couple of clever stories prepared that reinforce what you do and the value your company offers. Use humor to keep the stories interesting.

After the event, consider sending a handwritten note that references something interesting you learned about that person during your conversation. Handwritten notes are rarely used these days, which will make you stand out.

Your time is precious. Make the most of your next networking event by making yourself memorable.

MASTER THE BUSINESS LUNCH TO CONNECT

THE ART OF the successful business lunch is no longer a common skill among sales professionals, so mastering it will help set you apart in the marketplace. Call it old school, but the bottom line is that this strategy still works.

A business lunch affords you the unique opportunity to converse with your prospect for an hour or more in a captive setting where his guard is down. It's a rare chance to connect with your prospect personally, building personal rapport and trust.

While it might not seem appropriate to ask about a prospect's family in a traditional business meeting, for example, over lunch this topic seems natural. If your prospect is stalling on making a purchasing decision, a lunch meeting provides a perfect opportunity to get to the heart of the problem.

While there are many benefits to lunch meetings, many sales professionals remain uncomfortable with them. Instead, they gravitate toward the tried-and-true office meeting. Why? Engaging the prospect in a social setting opens the door for mistakes. However, there are several common mistakes that can be easily avoided, even in a more casual setting.

When proposing lunch, suggest restaurants close to your prospect with environments conducive to conversation and consistent with his personal style. Arrive early, and always take the best seat. Seating yourself in a prime location subtly communicates you're a person of value.

Sit with your back to the wall. You'll see your prospect arrive, and you'll also make sure that nothing distracts your prospect from the conversation. If he can see diners entering the restaurant, you're less likely to maintain his focus.

Turn your cell phone off and remove it from sight. Taking a phone call during lunch is a social sin, and leaving it on the table communicates that your prospect isn't your top priority.

You're not at lunch for the food. You're there to build a relationship and advance the sale. Eat something light ahead of time so you can focus more on what your prospect is saying and less on your food. When ordering, select an easy-to-eat dish.

Encourage your prospect to order first, and then follow his lead. If he orders a first-course salad, do the same so he's not eating alone.

Wait until after you've both ordered before talking business. Don't shortchange the small talk, as your primary purpose is to make a personal connection. While it's important to establish similar personal interests, you should always avoid one-upmanship.

Walk into the meeting with at least three personal questions and three business questions. Choose these questions strategically, so the answers can help you make a personal connection or help you advance the sale. This is your opportunity to ask tough questions like, "Tell me more about your relationship with your existing vendor."

A well-planned business lunch can help you quickly advance your relationship with a prospect and give you a leg up against your competition. Get out of your traditional meeting routine, and go have lunch.

GET LINKEDIN TO OPPORTUNITY

FOR MOST INDUSTRIES, relationships drive sales. It's all about whom you know, and more importantly, how you make them feel. LinkedIn has created efficiencies around both of these aspects of relationship building.

LinkedIn is the largest online professional network with more than 350 million registered users and 4 million businesses represented with company pages as of 2015. It's an immense database of professionals, along with their résumés. Information is standardized, and the search tool is robust, making it easier to find specific individuals on LinkedIn, especially compared with Facebook or Twitter.

LinkedIn also provides more comprehensive member profiles. If you're connected with someone, you may be able to view his entire résumé along with that of everyone else he's connected with.

LinkedIn enables you to make a first connection with a much larger group of prospects than you normally would through traditional offline networking. It also allows you to quickly prepare for a prospect meeting, finding possible connections to incorporate into your discussion, like common acquaintances, former employers or the schools you both attended.

Here are several ways you can maximize your personal LinkedIn profile.

Fill out your individual profile completely. If it's not 100 percent complete, be sure you've uploaded your photo, selected five or more skills, received endorsements from others, and have at least 50 connections. According to LinkedIn, having a profile photo makes your profile seven times more likely to be found in searches.

Unlike Twitter, where frequency is key, too many posts on LinkedIn can easily turn users off. With most business categories, two to three times a week is enough, and those status updates should stay focused on your business experiences by recalling lessons learned, sharing best practices or mentioning special projects your team is working on now.

Grow your network by joining targeted groups, then inviting those members to connect with you. This is an easy way to reach a broader group of prospects with your status updates.

Post original content to your LinkedIn blog. Drive traffic to that blog by engaging with those commenting on your blog post. It's also a good strategy to search for other similar posts within your network by simply typing keywords into the LinkedIn search window. Comment on their content and provide a link back to your blog post as an additional resource.

Get recommendations by giving them to others who may feel obliged to give you one in return.

You can also leverage the "Who's Viewed Your Profile" feature, found under the Profile navigation button, to gain key insight and demographics on those viewing your posts and profile. This reporting will even allow you to compare viewership and engagement for specific posts in comparison to others. Focus your content on what's delivering for you, whether that's team or product photos, demonstration videos, customer testimonials, informative educational content, or case studies that illustrate the results you've generated for your customers.

If you have business-to-business sales responsibilities, you simply can't afford to ignore the power of LinkedIn.

SIX EASY WAYS TO KICK REFERRAL FEARS

ESPECIALLY FOR COMPANIES that sell products or services to other businesses, there is no more efficient way to generate new business than through referrals from happy existing customers. If a happy client refers his friends, trust has already been built into the equation, which generally shortens the sales cycle. Additionally, there is typically very little cost associated with generating new business through referrals.

Why don't businesses rely on referral generation more heavily? It usually boils down to fear. Some people are afraid of appearing too "salesy;" others are afraid of seeming desperate for work. Some professionals just lack confidence, and they aren't sure that they deserve the referral.

If your confidence is the problem, you have to adjust your own mindset first. No business delivers complete perfection every time. Be fair to yourself, and make sure that your expectations for your business are realistic. If you still lack confidence, you may have some service opportunities. The most straightforward method for course correcting begins with asking customers what you could do to more fully deliver on their expectations.

Once you believe you've earned the right to ask for referrals, there are six easy ways to make referral generation a natural part of your relationship-building process with current clients.

Make sure you're having quarterly conversations with each of your customers, asking about what makes your company better than the competition, what you should do more often, and what you should stop doing. Tell them how you're going to act on that feedback. Next, explain that you're looking to grow your business. Name five specific businesses that you think could benefit most from doing business with your company, and explain your reasoning.

Make it easy for your customers to refer business to you. Teach them how to talk about your business by giving them insight into your elevator pitch.

Treat vendors and suppliers as partners, and actively refer business their way. If you send business to them, they will probably do the same for you.

Set the expectation for referrals upfront by telling new customers you intend to exceed their service expectations and that your business relies heavily on referrals.

Consider offering a referral incentive to customers for a limited time. If the incentive is open-ended, customers may file the offer away in the back of their minds, waiting for an opportunity to arise, ultimately forgetting entirely. Deadlines create a sense of urgency.

Explain how you would like to receive referrals. If your request is vague, your customer might think that the referral seems like too much work. Instead, keep the ball in your court. You might say, "I will send you a template of an email that you can customize before you send it to the prospect. Be sure to CC me. I'll take it from there."

When a customer does refer a prospect your way, be sure to follow up with a phone call — or even an old-fashioned handwritten thank-you note.

STOP ASKING FOR REFERRALS

REFERRED PROSPECTS OFFER one of the strongest returns of any marketing or sales strategy you can deploy. After all, a good referral costs nothing upfront, and a referred prospect is much more likely to become a customer than most average leads.

Why do most companies have inconsistent referral-generation strategies, then? Reasons often include not knowing how to broach the subject or just being fearful of forcing an awkward conversation with a good client.

If having a traditional referral conversation is just not in your wheelhouse, try a new approach. Stop asking. Instead, enhance the natural process that clients and influencers use to offer referrals.

Here's an example of one way to approach influencers in your market. Let's say you sell custom pools, and you're targeting a colleague at a landscaping company. Explain the type of customers you can help the most, and get specific. For example, you might say you do your best work with owners of custom homes, who have an average annual income above $300K, who have kids, and are seeking an outside living space featuring a unique pool experience versus just a traditional pool. The more specific you are, the easier it will be for influencers to remember what you do.

Next, help them understand that by doing that type of custom work, you routinely get requests for landscapers. Ask them who their ideal customers are, so when someone asks about landscaping, you know if that prospect is a good fit. Positioning the conversation from their perspective gives you an opening to talk about what you do. However, make sure you follow through by referring prospective customers to them.

When it comes to asking your customers to refer prospects to you, have regular check-in conversations in which you ask about what you do that they find most valuable and what you should stop doing. Explain you're working to grow your business, and ask them how they would recommend getting the word out about the specialized work that you do.

By asking in this casual way, you're avoiding a potentially uncomfortable conversation where your customer might be unable to quickly think of a prospective client for your company. By asking him to brainstorm with you, you are engaging him in a deeper way, increasing the likelihood he will remember your differentiators, and that will help keep your desire for referrals top of mind.

When a customer does refer a prospect your way, be sure to follow up with a handwritten thank-you note. An email is just not as thoughtful, and it's likely to get buried in an inbox.

STOP BARGAINING; START NEGOTIATING

MOST BUSINESS PROFESSIONALS have taken a class or read a book to sharpen their negotiating skills. Unfortunately, what's often taught is how to bargain, not how to negotiate — and the two couldn't be more different. Bargaining is about determining who is right, but negotiating is about determining what is right.

If you're fighting for who is right, someone always loses. Why would a new customer of yours, who just felt beaten down through bargaining, want to work with your firm long-term? You may win this time, but what are the odds that the customer will buy again by renewing his agreement with you? Do you think she would ever refer your company to a friend or colleague?

One nationally recognized expert on the art of negotiation, Jack Kaine, is a hired gun recruited by corporations across the globe for his counsel during tough business negotiations. His negotiating philosophy is that, in order for both parties to win, you must enlarge the pie, not divide it. That can mean simply adding value to what you're bringing to the table, not just cutting your price.

Let's say you sell luxury automobiles and a regular customer of yours is going to buy from the dealership in a nearby city because its cost is five percent lower. Especially given that you're selling an upscale product, the last thing you want to do is discount the price. If you do, you're encouraging your customers to bargain with you.

Instead, ask if the competing dealership offers free oil changes for life as well as loaner cars if you ever need a repair. If that doesn't close the deal, you might also offer free tires for life, knowing that most high-end car buyers sell their vehicles long before they ever need new tires. The idea is that the perceived value in what you've added to the negotiation is high, but your actual cost is much lower than the 5 percent discount requested. You've also maintained the integrity of your price.

It's important that you look at yourself as a problem-solver, not just a negotiator. You are there to ask the right questions that uncover what the other party needs to feel satisfied, ultimately finding a way to deliver that satisfaction, even if it's in an entirely unexpected way.

Don't just focus on winning. Instead, walk away with a deal that works for both parties.

TEN NO-NONSENSE NEGOTIATING STRATEGIES

THERE ARE NEGOTIATION STRATEGIES that build relationships, instead of tearing the other side down. It's not enough to win the negotiation if you're damaging the relationship in the process. In fact, customers that feel beaten down through the negotiation process may become disgruntled and consider competitors at their next opportunity. Instead of winning at all costs, focus on creating a mutually beneficial deal.

Adopt this philosophy and deploy these negotiating strategies to close more win/win deals.

Prepare for the negotiation by jotting down your perceptions and assumptions about the other party and the negotiation. Next, write down how you imagine the other party perceives things, allowing yourself to see both sides of the playbook ahead of time.

The person who speaks first sets the tone for the negotiation. Script your opening statement word for word to make sure it demonstrates strength while also emphasizing your openness to finding a mutually beneficial solution.

The person who asks the most questions determines the direction of the negotiation. Ask more "what" than "why" questions to steer the conversation toward more fact-based reasoning.

Never argue, but always ask questions for understanding. If a prospect says, "That price is too high," surprise him by agreeing in this way. "You're right. This is a lot of money. Perhaps I've included some services you don't need, or some that you could do yourself." Ask clarifying questions, and then offer to return later with itemized pricing, which should net a higher total, demonstrating the value of packaged pricing.

People do things for their reasons, not yours. Find out what the other person wants, and then help him get it.

The person who listens best will have the greatest influence over the outcome.

Do not bargain with yourself by cutting costs before you present your proposal to a client, or you'll be making unasked-for concessions for which you won't get credit. Real bargainers won't buy without a concession of some kind, so build one into your proposal behind the scenes.

If you know your prospect is going to have a concern, lead with it. Include it in your opening remarks to effectively level the playing field.

If you aren't sure the other person wants to find a workable solution, pay more attention to his feet than his words. If he isn't headed for the door, he is still interested.

Never make a concession the minute you know you can and unless you can explain what new information you have that justifies the change, or else you'll lose credibility. Instead, slow down the negotiation, explaining that you'll get back to the prospect.

Ultimately, the best negotiating strategy is to maintain a strong balance sheet and very satisfied clients. Having a strong back-up plan sets you free to make good decisions for your company.

FIVE TOP SALES NEGOTIATION MISTAKES

MORE THAN 75 PERCENT of the sales reps I have coached through the years cite price as their number one objection. Given the tumultuous state of our economy, that's no surprise. Even when the economy is in a better place, however, one side effect of a recession is the bargaining mindset that it creates in the market.

It's a reality that sales professionals everywhere face, so it is vital to sharpen your sales negotiation skills. Improve your sales performance by avoiding these five common negotiating mistakes.

Mistake #1: Not asking enough questions. The person who asks the most questions in a sales negotiation ultimately charts the direction for that conversation. Don't ask why. Instead, you should ask "what" questions to encourage your prospect to focus on the facts.

Mistake #2: Discounting emotions in a negotiation. While it's certainly advisable not to react emotionally in a negotiation, emotions do play a factor. The key is to manage your prospect's emotions by building trust. Prospects that feel understood, engaged and valued are more likely to trust you, which paves the way for a rational decision about your proposal.

Mistake #3: Bargaining with yourself. Don't cut costs before you ever present your proposal to the prospect. If you encounter a prospect that's a bargainer, he often won't buy without some sort of concession. If you make all those concessions behind the scenes, though, your prospect won't see your flexibility during the negotiation.

Mistake #4: Bargaining instead of negotiating. Instead of cutting your price, add something of value to your proposal. Look at yourself as a problem solver, not just a negotiator. Your role is to ask the right questions to find out what the other party needs to feel satisfied with the negotiation and then to find a unique way to deliver what the prospect needs. Come prepared with a few ideas that add value without also adding a hard cost to the equation.

Mistake #5: Responding immediately to an objection. When prospects raise an objection, they're often hinting at hidden issues. If you immediately address each objection, you may gloss over their hidden concerns and lose the sale without ever knowing why. When your prospect throws out an objection to the cost, for example, consider saying, "I can tell this an important concern, and rightfully so. Tell me more about your hesitation with cost." What you may find is that your prospect isn't concerned about cash flow, but he is worried about the return he will see on his investment.

Avoiding these common sales negotiation mistakes will help you close more deals, while still forging strong relationships along the way.

AVOID THESE SEVEN DEADLY SALES SINS

WHETHER YOU CALL IT SALES, business development or fundraising, bringing in new customers or donors is essential to your organization's growth. After all, as the late founder of IBM, Thomas Watson, so prolifically stated, "Nothing happens until someone sells something."

However, there are seven deadly sales sins that everyone needs to avoid to be successful.

Assuming great work leads to loyalty: Don't mistake a paying customer for a loyal one. Perceptions of value can vary between vendor and customer. If you're doubting the unwavering loyalty of your customers, ask them what more you could be doing to exceed expectations.

Assuming clients will refer others to you: Even if they're completely satisfied with your work, your customers won't necessarily refer your company to others. Instead, take your clients to lunch a couple times a year to gauge their satisfaction, and to inquire about their changing business needs. Not only does this present an opportunity to suggest other products or services that may be a good fit, but it is also an ideal time to involve them in your referral process.

Not building bench strength: Investing all of your time in a single relationship is always risky. If your contact moves on, you could be at the mercy of a new manager who wants new partnerships. Savvy sales professionals develop relationships with multiple people at each organization, even if those people are still sitting on the bench for now.

Not understanding the decision-making process: Even veteran sales professionals can be reluctant to ask about a prospect's decision-making process, including others who may influence the purchasing decision. You have every right to ask these questions early in the relationship.

Discounting without cause: If discounting is your go-to sales strategy, you're telling prospects you lack confidence in the value you're offering. If you've demonstrated your value, and you've built trust with a prospect, and you're competitively priced, discounting shouldn't be necessary. If it's absolutely necessary, make a small concession that you can justify (e.g., reduced scope of a project or fewer bells and whistles on the product), so the prospect understands this isn't typical.

Only calling when you need something: Be sure you're not only calling prospects when you need a sale. Good relationships aren't one-sided. Read the news, and follow your customer's industry. Keep tabs on what their competitors are doing. You should consider inviting your customers to any networking events or educational talks that they might find beneficial.

Assuming you're born with sales skills: Selling is a learned skill. It requires effort, discipline and a lot of practice — just like anything that's worth mastering. Remember that failure often leads to innovation. Even if you don't knock it out of the park every time, your team can still round the bases.

TOP REASONS SALESPEOPLE FIND FAILURE

JUST LIKE there are some fundamental skills that can make a sales professional successful regardless of the industry he represents, there are also clear, universal reasons that prevent salespeople from achieving peak performance. In fact, the Harvard Business Review reports that only one in three working salespeople is "consistently effective," with only one out of 250 exceeding their targets. Here are five common reasons that many sales professionals find themselves not quite hitting the mark.

Lack of discipline: Sales is a numbers game. The key to success is to develop an activity plan, and stick to your plan every day. Start your day with the toughest task, the one you dread the most. If that dreaded task is cold calling, start your calls as soon as you walk in the door and don't stop until you have set the number of meetings you're targeting. After that, the rest of the day will be a piece of cake.

Failure to leverage happy clients: Every quarter, invite your happiest clients to lunch individually. Find out what you can do to improve their experience, and then collaborate with them to brainstorm how you can collectively reach out to the people they know who need your services.

Fear of determining real buying intentions: Too often, salespeople avoid asking the hard questions that ultimately qualify or disqualify a prospect, especially when it comes to tricky topics like the prospect's intentions and ability to buy. Asking these questions early in the sales process helps you avoid spinning your wheels.

Presenting instead of listening: Roughly 7 out of 10 salespeople kick off a new prospect meeting by diving straight into a pitch. Instead, start by listening. Ask open-ended, high-impact questions to learn what matters to your prospects, and then adapt your pitch accordingly. Prospects are more inclined to buy when they feel like they've been heard, and you might also be able to identify additional selling opportunities.

Needing to convince clients, instead of solving problems: Great salespeople don't walk into every sale assuming the prospect has a need for their products or services. Instead, the objective is to ask good questions and learn what's important to each individual prospect. If the prospect needs your services and you qualify him as a good customer, that's great. If not, see if there are other problems you can solve for that prospect, and you'll be creating a loyal referral source in the process.

SURE-FIRE WAYS TO KILL A SALE

TODAY'S BUSINESS CLIMATE is tough for sales professionals. When good prospects are few and far between, putting your best foot forward in each sales pitch becomes crucial to your survival. Given this reality, avoid these most common sales missteps to ensure you make the most of each prospect opportunity.

One common mistake is telling, not selling. Selling is all about listening. Eager salespeople have a tendency to share too much, talking about every product feature and benefit before they really understand the prospect's needs. Instead of talking over your prospect, ask questions to identify the challenges the prospect is facing. Resist the temptation to talk much until you've conducted a thorough needs assessment and are ready to tell the prospect how you can solve the problem or address his needs.

Talking at your prospects is another common mistake. Good sales professionals know how to engage a prospect, creating a dynamic and interactive conversation. They carefully watch their prospects, adapting the conversation based on each prospect's verbal and non-verbal cues.

Some sales professionals seem not to hear what prospects are actually saying. If you're not properly prepared for a sales pitch, you might miss key details a prospect shares because you're focused on what you're going to say next. Prepare enough in advance so you can relax and really listen. Be in the moment. This will allow you to reflect on what your prospect has shared and comment thoughtfully, building rapport along the way.

Accepting superficial answers can be a stumbling block, too. When asked tough questions, prospects may use evasive maneuvers in lieu of providing real, candid answers. Recognize this, and don't be afraid to probe further. Let's say you ask a prospect about his relationship with an existing vendor and the response is, "For the most part, it's okay." Recognize that he has just hinted at a possible weakness, and ask a fearless follow-up question by saying, "Tell me more about what could be improved."

Other sales professionals seem desperate. Prospects can sense when you need the sale more than they need your products or services. Desperation can make you reckless, deafening your senses. Instead, think clearly about the value you're offering the prospect. Recognize that not every prospect is going to be a good fit for your company, and walk into a sales meeting with the mindset that you're there to determine if the prospect is a good fit for you.

Talking in platitudes is another common misstep for sales professionals. Make sure you have something substantial to contribute to the conversation. When prospects gain new, relevant knowledge through your interactions, you'll build credibility in their eyes, which makes them more likely to take your proposal seriously.

Finally, remember that there's no reason to try reading a prospect's mind. When you get a negative response, don't assume price is the issue. In fact, don't make assumptions at all. Try saying, "Tell me more about your hesitation in moving forward." If your prospect does cite price as an issue, ask what other concerns he has. Often, if you can resolve his other concerns, price becomes less important.

ASSUMPTIONS THAT COST YOU SALES

GOOD SALES PROFESSIONALS are experts on the products and services they sell. This expertise inevitably creates a few blind spots. When you feel like you've seen it all — every prospect response, motivation and objection — it's easy to occasionally jump to the wrong conclusion.

It's not realistic to assume your customers will remember most of what you tell them. Research shows customers forget 50 percent of your conversation within an hour, and 90 percent after just one week. Instead, focus the conversation around your prospect. The more the prospect talks about himself, the more he'll remember the connection you made with him. Use open-ended questions to encourage him to talk more about challenges that your products and services can help solve. If the prospect sees the need for your products or services on his own, he is more likely to remember that need after you're gone. Secondly, narrow your message down to a few key points that resonate with your prospect, and refer to them frequently throughout your conversation.

If you assume that every prospect is the right prospect, you are setting yourself up for failure. Instead, when you walk into a prospect meeting, remember that you aren't yet sure if this prospect is ideal for your company. You are there to make a mutual decision about a partnership. If it isn't a good fit, walk away.

Your time is too valuable to invest in a low-probability sale or one from a customer that isn't an ideal fit for your company.

Just having a need for your products or services doesn't mean that the prospect is motivated to make a purchase now. If the pain or need isn't severe, you may be looking at a long sales cycle — or spending too much time attempting to shorten the process. Don't hesitate to say, "It sounds like solving this problem isn't critical for you at this time. I'd like to propose that we meet again in six months to reassess your situation."

Don't assume you fully understand your prospect's question. Questions are often just objections in disguise. Instead, acknowledge that the question is clearly an important one, and then ask for more clarification to uncover any hidden objections.

Last but not least, never assume a prospect will call when he's ready to buy. He may be ready, but then he gets caught up in other issues and forgets about you entirely — or your competition may follow up before you do, stealing your sale and benefiting from all the work you've done. Following up should always be a priority.

Don't jump to conclusions. Just ask.

TOP FIVE SALES EXCUSES

GREAT SALES PROFESSIONALS have the ability to adapt based on the audience. They are able to embrace rejection as an express pass to their next "yes," and they generally have a high degree of emotional intelligence. However, even veteran sales professionals can fall into the trappings of making excuses as a way to cope with the hurdles they encounter during the sales process.

There are five common sales excuses that may sometimes seem most tempting, but learning how to overcome them can ensure you continue to sell at the top of your game.

Our prices are too high: There will always be a cheaper competitor, and it's true that prospects care about price. However, price is rarely the final factor. Take price off the table. Sell value instead, helping your prospect focus on what you can uniquely deliver.

The economy is bad: It's true that it may never look like 2007 again, but companies are still making purchasing decisions. Identify those companies, and then target them. What unique pain can your products or services alleviate for them? How can you tell when a company needs your products or services? Finding those trigger points can create tremendous sales efficiency, ensuring that you're spending the bulk of your time focused on qualified buyers who aren't letting the economy interfere with making good business decisions.

No one returns my voicemails: High-level decision makers are inundated with sales and marketing messages. If your voicemail lacks a compelling reason to return the call, it's not worth the time you invested in leaving it. Before you leave a message, conduct research to find a connection or compelling reason your prospect should return your call; but in the end, it's worth remembering that the phone is just one of many sales tools available.

My sales goals aren't realistic: On the surface, it may seem like it's impossible to step up your game every year, but strong sales professionals constantly evaluate themselves so that they can improve. Self-evaluation can lead to greater efficiency and stronger sales performance.

It's all whom you know: Relationships make such a difference in the sales profession, so why not go network, allowing your relationship-building skills to expand your reach? If you network enough in your market, there will come a time when you're almost always able to secure a warm introduction to an ideal prospect.

Even the best sales professionals can lose sales, but these losses don't define your potential. It's how you react to the loss that shows your true character. By recognizing what went wrong and how you can improve your game next time, you'll separate yourself from the pack.

SUSTAINED GROWTH REQUIRES A SELLING CULTURE

IN THE EARLY DAYS of a small business, the founders typically have to become rainmakers. However, as their businesses grow, owners often struggle with how to impart their passion for sales to others, so that the whole team can work together to sustain growth.

If you want to create a scalable business model that doesn't depend on one or two people to bring in new business, you will have to create a company-wide sales culture first, where every member of the team takes part in sales in some way, and where the role of sales isn't negatively perceived. After all, if no sales are closing, there's no business to go around.

The most straightforward way to create a sales culture is to ensure that employees have a stake in company performance. Profit-sharing programs or bonuses that are tied to company performance can be the most important centerpiece in any sales culture. Communicate your sales goals to employees. Let them understand how they can each contribute to those goals. Show them what they can earn when they reach those goals.

Find a role for everyone. Not everyone has the chops for cold calling, but there are sales process roles suited to everyone within your company — from researching a prospect to preparing for the sales team's first meeting. Maybe one of your employees would be great at finding highly personalized birthday gifts to give to your top customers and prospects. Even handwriting thank-you notes to customers celebrating anniversaries with your firm can be an important assignment.

Truly empower your employees to take care of your customers. Show them how much more expensive it is to attract a new customer than it is to maintain an existing one.

Teach your employees how to cross-sell, upsell and generate referrals from existing customers. Proper training will make sure your team experiences "wins" along the way, which are critical to maintaining team enthusiasm around supporting the sales process and reaching targets.

Role-play selling scenarios. Even though this can be intimidating at first, it can also be one of the most effective tools in helping your team prepare for real-world opportunities.

Lead by example. Culture change begins at the top. Walk the walk. Make sales calls. Shadow your team on sales calls. Incorporate the topic of sales into your regular staff meetings. Publicly recognize top sales performers — both those in out-front, full-time sales roles as well as those in behind-the-scenes sales support roles.

Hold your entire team accountable for sales activity, not just revenue. While we may not be able to fully control when someone signs a contract or writes a check, what we can control is the number of people we approach and therefore get in front of each week. Regularly coach your team for improved performance. Consistency is key.

If you want to see your business sustain growth even when you're not in a primary business development role, invest time in creating a company-wide sales culture.

DEVELOPING A REPEATABLE SALES PROCESS

IT'S TRUE THAT "nothing happens until someone sells something," as aptly said by IBM's founder Thomas Watson. However, if you talk to business owners about identifying a predictable, repeatable sales process that ensures their teams consistently meet sales targets, they look at you like you're talking about the Holy Grail — enticing, but always elusive.

What exactly is a repeatable sales process? It's a formula for how you sell, starting from the very first conversation and continuing until the deal is closed, including all the steps along the way.

For example, you would need to know the answers to questions like these: What are your most predictable and effective forms of lead generation — advertising, networking, cold calling or referrals? Do you use the same qualification process each time? Which questions work best in that very first conversation with a prospect? Do you go through the same buying process with each new prospect? How do you follow up after those first conversations in a way that creates results, and do you have a proven template for those messages?

To create a repeatable sales process, start by taking an educated guess at the most effective formula, documenting it fully. Create a flowchart of each step in the process, with variations for inbound and outbound leads, since they often look quite different.

Next, create scripts, templates and tools to automate the process for your team so everyone can easily replicate it and measure the accuracy of your predictions. After all, you can't measure what works — apples to apples, across your team — without any consistency. Try it for at least 30 days, as outlined, and document your conversion rate.

Next, tear your blueprint apart, one tiny piece at a time, to improve your conversion rate. You might, for example, take something as small as the follow-up email sent after a first prospect meeting. Work to enhance it, adding value for your prospect, with an eye on increasing receptivity in your next meeting.

Only work to revamp a single step at a time, and then test the refined sales process for roughly 30 days with the change in place. By isolating a single change at a time, you will be able to accurately measure the impact of that change on your overall sales process.

If you identify a significant bottleneck in your process — like only 20 percent of prospects you deliver a proposal to agree to buy, for example — use your resources to improve that part of the process. Consider offering an incentive to the member of your team who fixes the problem.

With a repeatable sales process in hand, you can easily create a scalable sales model for your growing business.

HOW TO SPOT GREAT SALES TALENT

SALES SKILLS CAN BE TAUGHT. It's a myth that successful salespeople are born to sell. In reality, sales skills are learned, crafted and honed through years of practice.

However, there are inherent personality traits that signal a sales professional is destined for greatness. When interviewing sales professionals, look for these traits. Everything else — closing skills, the ability to overcome objections, conducting an effective needs assessment — can be taught later.

Determination: Having the ability to focus and pursue objectives with an inner sense of drive is essential in sales.

Listening: High-performing sales professionals have extraordinary listening skills. Not only do they recognize the importance of encouraging a prospect to open up, but they also pick up on nonverbal cues. They are able to see where a prospect's hesitation lies because they have strong intuition. During the interview, let the conversation fall silent to see how they handle it. If they scramble to fill the void, they aren't for you.

Financial motivation: The best sales professionals are typically motivated by money. If they ask financial questions in the preliminary interview, that's a good sign.

Preparation: Good salespeople embrace the importance of preparation. During your interview, double-check to make sure they did their homework. If they didn't, move on to your next candidate. If they aren't disciplined enough to prepare for a job interview, what are the odds they will prepare for every meeting with ideal prospects?

Rapport: When the candidate walked into your office, did he establish a connection with you? Did he work to uncover a common interest? If he didn't, he might not connect with prospects on a sales call either.

Confidence: Top sales performers are unlikely to feel self-conscious about much on a sales call, or during an interview.

Humility: Even though confidence is key, it has to be balanced with a sense of modesty. Without humility, prospects may think this sales professional is condescending to them, killing the deal.

Achievement Oriented: Great salespeople like to exceed targets. Give them goals and the tools to achieve them, and then let them go.

Moderate Friendliness: Top sales performers are not typically the most gregarious in the bunch. An extreme degree of friendliness may actually work against a sales professional that ought to be listening to prospects, patiently driving them toward a sale.

Sense of Duty: Successful sales professionals have an unwavering sense of duty toward their work, and they love to generate results.

Hiring the right sales talent is perhaps the most challenging of all recruiting tasks, but it's vital. There is an art to making the right choice, and even then, 50 percent of those you hire are likely not to work out. Improve your odds by making sure your top pick has all of these traits.

AMBIVERTS MAKE SALES ROCK STARS

MOST BUSINESS OWNERS and hiring managers struggle to find good sales talent, but I would contend that's because many are simply focusing on the wrong candidate profile.

It's a common stereotype that the strongest extroverts make the best sales professionals. Everyone has experienced their fair share of highly extroverted salespeople in their lifetimes — ones who talked so much, you couldn't get a word in edgewise and whose aggressive style was such a turnoff that it ultimately prevented you from buying.

A 2012 study, called "Rethinking the Extroverted Sales Ideal" and published by Adam Grant in Psychological Science, indicates that the people who are the best at sales usually have a completely different personality type.

They're called "ambiverts," and they are essentially equal parts extrovert and introvert. That balance equates to an innate versatility — and an invaluable sales trait.

The study draws conclusions from the performance records of 340 outbound salespeople. Ambiverts outperformed their introvert and extrovert counterparts by 23 and 32 percent, respectively. Why? Ambiverts have an instinctively flexible communication style, so they are able to more easily match the style of their prospects. They balance the desire to talk with the need to listen, and as a result, they avoid the appearance of overconfidence. However, they also demonstrate the assertiveness and enthusiasm necessary to close a sale.

Another interesting study finding is that extreme introverts and extroverts perform at virtually the same level — most likely because the most critical skill in sales is the ability to listen. Introverts more frequently possess strong listening skills, which can make up for any deficiencies in more extroverted qualities like building rapport or closing the sale.

How do you identify an ambivert in a sales candidate interview? Ask your candidate to rate these 10 questions on a scale of one to five where one is strongly agree and five is strongly disagree. You're looking for an average of all the responses that falls in the middle.

1. I prefer one-on-one conversations to group activities.

2. I'm a big risk taker.

3. I prefer to express myself in writing (versus verbally).

4. I enjoy solitude.

5. People tell me I've never met a stranger.

6. People describe me as soft spoken.

7. I am most energized when I'm around other people.

8. I prefer work that allows me to "dive in" with few interruptions.

9. I prefer to work alone.

10. In sales pitches, I'm good at "shooting from the hip."

You probably already know whether your sales team falls on the introverted or extroverted side of the scale. Compare this information against the team's performance to see if this study holds true inside your organization — and if so, consider an ambivert for your next sales position.

RIGHT-BRAINED REPS IN A LEFT-BRAINED WORLD

ACCORDING TO ALBERT EINSTEIN, the definition of insanity is "doing the same thing over and over again and expecting a different result." However, it's still common for sales managers to feel like they're beating their heads against the wall trying to get their sales professionals to follow established processes to manage orders and track progress. While this is frustrating for managers, it can be equally frustrating for their sales professionals, too.

Most of the time, the root cause of the conflict is that the very traits you sought in hiring your sales team — relationship building, intuition and innovation — may be at odds with the skills required to efficiently manage administrative tasks, like organization, follow-through and technical skills. Many right-brained sales reps are working in a world full of left-brained processes that haven't been created with their inherent strengths in mind.

Before you make any assumptions about your sales team and its inherent strengths, consider administering a test to assess each member of your team's thinking preferences. There are many options available for assessing left-brain and right-brain tendencies, with one of the more common being the Herrmann Brain Dominance Instrument or HBDI.

Whether your sales professionals are left-brained or right-brained, they still have the ability to leverage both sides of their brains — but their natural tendencies will always be to play toward their strengths. It takes a concerted effort for a shift from one side of the brain to the other. Instead of pushing the boulder uphill, consider redesigning your sales processes to ease the burden on your sales team and allow team members to focus on what they do best — selling. If you have a predominantly right-brained sales team, conduct a quick assessment of your top sales processes and adapt them accordingly.

If you have a Customer Relationship Management (CRM) tool in place, consider customizing it by removing all fields that are less than vital. Where possible, try to limit the data required for entry for a new prospect to 10 fields or less, removing all of the clutter.

If you have sales professionals out in the field, you'll want the order entry process to be as streamlined and efficient as possible, both to reduce the amount of time it takes to place an order and to reduce errors. While this may mean investing in technology and software, consider the savings realized when you no longer need someone on your team to follow-up with customers, reviewing and finalizing each order.

Leveraging the strengths of your sales professionals and providing them the tools they need to efficiently stay organized will create a win/win outcome for your entire team.

SIX REVEALING SALES INTERVIEW QUESTIONS

THE NEW HIRE FAILURE RATE is astonishing and expensive — and it's even worse for sales candidates, who can be among the toughest job applicants to properly evaluate. Leadership IQ reports that of 20,000 new hires tracked in a recent study, 46 percent failed within 18 months.

Many people blame ineffective interviews, because if you aren't asking the right questions, you won't get the insights you need. Barrett Riddleberger, CEO of xPotential Selling, has suggested that there are a handful of quality questions (positioned here as statements) we should all ask our next sales candidate.

"Tell me how you defined a qualified buyer in your prior sales role and how, specifically, you arrived at that determination." Candidates that can't successfully map this out for you are likely to waste their time chasing low-potential prospects. Strong responses will touch on the profile of ideal targeted buyer including demographics and oftentimes psychographics, budget alignment, and the fact that the ideal customer has needs you can actually meet.

"Tell me about one of your most successful sales calls over the past month, including the approach you took, how the conversation flowed, and the outcome." You're seeking clarity that the sales rep uses a consultative approach based on high-impact questions that identify the prospect's needs and make him feel understood. You're also looking for a sales professional with a clear game plan for each sales call. If your candidate is shooting from the hip in his response, his approach to prospect meetings is likely equally laissez-faire.

"Tell me about the last book you read on sales and the two big ideas with which you walked away." Specifically how and where did you implement them and with what degree of success? This question will reveal a candidate's attitude about ongoing development and how the candidate might respond to coaching.

"Tell me specifically how you found leads to fill your pipeline during your first 90 days in your previous role." If you need a hunter who can identify his own leads, then you're looking for a proactive method that's sufficient to keep the pipeline full. If the candidate's response is that he asks for referrals from existing customers, your follow-up questions might include: How many referral conversations do you have a month? How many new sales do you target a month? How many new prospects must you put into your funnel each month to reach that target? Figure out whether the candidate's sales-funnel assumptions seem realistic.

"Think back to your last experience talking with a gatekeeper. Tell me about the language you used with him or her." If you want a hunter, his response to this question should be well rehearsed, since he probably delivers it several times every day, to the point where it doesn't sound scripted.

"Think about your largest account that you brought in on your own in your prior sales role. Tell me how that first meeting went and why you deemed it successful. Now provide a similar account of a prospect you weren't able to land. Tell me about that first meeting. What, if anything, would you do differently?" You're looking for candidates that want to become a trusted advisor and gather enough information to determine next steps, even if that sometimes means walking away. If the candidate is too obsessed with closing every single deal, and winning at all costs, he is not likely for you. But you do want to hear that he progresses the sale, ask for the business where appropriate, and follow up where necessary.

In the end, recruiting sales talent is still mostly an art — but with these questions, you can start to understand what really makes each candidate tick.

USE EQ VS. IQ TO RECRUIT SALES TALENT

HIRING SALES TALENT IS TRICKY, as it can be difficult to distinguish between those who are merely strong at interviewing and those who will actually be strong on the job. Why? Sales people are particularly good at reading people and delivering the desired response. The trick is to peel back the onion during an interview to ensure you are getting an unfiltered view of each candidate, which can be done by combining two techniques.

The first is behavioral interviewing, which is based on the premise that a person's past performance is the best indication of future performance. As such, candidates are asked to provide specific, real-life examples of how they handled and behaved in situations likely to arise in the new position. Instead of merely asking a candidate traditional questions related to job responsibilities, the interviewer might ask about a specific time the candidate had to flex his style to adapt to a client or for the candidate to share a particular example of when he had to persuade co-workers. Strong candidates will be able to easily provide detailed examples.

It's not enough to simply ask questions using this style of interviewing. For the full picture of a sales candidate under consideration, you must also gauge his ability to perceive, evaluate and appropriately respond to the emotions of others. It's called Emotional Intelligence or EQ for short, and many researchers believe it's far more important than IQ.

To ensure your new sales hires have a strong EQ, look for these three qualities according to Rain Group and SalesLeadership, Inc., but be sure to leverage behavioral interviewing techniques to gauge the degree to which candidates have them.

Delayed Gratification: Candidates with this quality aren't likely to give up before reaching a complex goal — such as the pursuit of large accounts. They are willing to put in the work to get the reward. Those struggling in this area aren't likely to stick with executing the daily tasks necessary to keep a sales pipeline filled. When instant gratification isn't achieved, they may lose focus entirely or spend most of their time checking in on existing customers as a feel-good exercise.

Empathy: Empathetic sales professionals can demonstrate that they see the world from their prospects' perspective, allowing them to quickly build trust. After all, what prospects want most is to feel understood.

Assertiveness: The assertive sales professional is able to ask tough questions without an aggressive tone. When a prospect uses a stall tactic such as, "let me think about it," the assertive sales professional might respond in this way. "This is such an important decision, and I can fully appreciate your desire to give it careful consideration. Tell me more about your hesitation."

Recruit better candidates by leveraging behavioral interviewing techniques and focusing on emotional skills.

GETTING WHAT YOU PAY FOR

WHAT SHOULD YOU DO if you have a unique product or service, and a solid sales team supporting it, but you still aren't realizing your company's potential? How can that happen? Often, your compensation plan is not encouraging the right sales approach, or even worse, it may be draining the motivation from your sales team. Changing your compensation structure can reward the right behaviors, boosting your bottom line.

Step One: Establish a Total Compensation Target

First, find out what your competitors are paying their top performers. Next, identify what ideal total compensation target you want your top sales reps to reach — their ideal total base and variable pay combined. Ideally, your top sales professionals who are hitting 100 percent of their targets should earn at least what the market is paying elsewhere — or even more.

Step Two: Determine the Compensation Mix

Your sales cycle, market maturity, and the type of sales position all play a role in determining the ideal mix between base and variable pay. If your sales cycle is long — usually taking six months or a year, for example — combine a high percentage of base pay with less variable pay, or establish a salary guarantee to ensure a new rep can make a living while building his sales pipeline. If you have a shorter sales cycle, lean more heavily toward commissions.

Remember that the type of sales position you're offering is also an important factor. Are you hiring "farmers" to maintain and up-sell existing customers, or are you looking for "hunters" to track down new business? Hunters are generally comfortable with high commission-based compensation plans, while farmers prefer a more predictable compensation model with a higher degree of base salary.

Step Three: Decide on Performance Measures

Next, determine the goals you need your sales team to reach. Generally, in newer markets, companies pay based on a percentage of total revenue a sales professional generates. In established markets, previous sales benchmarks make it easier to set specific sales quotas.

Another way to approach performance measures is to establish a short list of goals which could be a combination of revenue generated, sales quotas met, new prospect activity, profit margins earned, or even volume of a specific new product sold. Prioritize goals, and weight them in increasing importance. You should also consider including a component based on management discretion to reward performance factors that are hard to quantifiably measure.

Step Four: Establish a Payment Formula and Parameters

In creating your compensation formula, consider setting a minimum commission threshold so that each sales professional generates enough business to cost-justify his base salary before earning commissions. You might also integrate a "stretch goal" that significantly increases the sales rep's commission once the goal is met.

Step Five: Conduct Modeling

Finally, apply your proposed new comp plan to your sales team's actual performance during the last two years. How would the team have faired under the new plan compared to the old one?

If your sales team isn't reaching sales targets, look at your compensation plan. Remember, in more ways than one, you get what you pay for.

ARE SALESPEOPLE BORN OR MADE?

"IS GREATNESS BORN – OR IS IT MADE?" It's an age-old question, but in my view, greatness can be made — especially in sales. While sales skills can be taught, the learning curve is shorter for candidates with two key character traits: empathy and drive.

The best salespeople believe they are fulfilling need; they aren't just pushing a product. They have an uncanny ability to identify a prospect's needs by asking probing questions, connecting emotionally with the prospect while they explain how their products or services can uniquely solve the prospect's problem.

Sales professionals that ask strong questions, and then listen intently to the answers, have mastered the art of empathy. An empathetic sales professional shows customers that he cares and understands, connecting with the prospect emotionally by the end of a call.

The drive to succeed is equally important. Driven sales professionals have no fear of rejection. They won't hesitate to ask for the business, and they are persistent at overcoming a prospect's hesitancy to buy. They are self-motivated to attain financial targets.

Without empathy, though, having sales professionals who are too driven can result in lost customers and prospects that walk away feeling pushed toward a product that may not have actually solved their problems.

While drive and empathy are more difficult to learn, most of the other important sales skills are easy to teach. If you can find a candidate, however, who has already mastered these five essential, yet trainable, sales skills, you should be sure to catch that talent while you can.

Rapport Building: The ability to quickly connect with strangers is an undeniable asset. While many salespeople do it naturally, others can be trained on building rapport.

Organization and Follow-Through: Great sales professionals have exceptional organizational and follow-through skills that let them manage a territory efficiently.

Preparation: Great sales people avoid "winging it." Instead, they prepare before making each sales call, familiarizing themselves with their prospects ahead of time. Preparation allows them to map out a game plan in advance.

Effective Communication: Don't be surprised if your best sales professionals seem quiet when they're conducting sales calls. Instead of talking a mile a minute, they concentrate on what the prospect is saying, catching important buying cues and uncovering a need they can solve. They ask thoughtful follow-up questions, and they are respectful of others' opinions. They are also likely to communicate well in writing.

Discipline: The best sales professionals approach selling with discipline, setting a schedule that they can commit to every day. Despite the freedom that comes with a sales job, they have figured out how to stay focused so they can maximize their results.

If your sales team could stand to strengthen these skills, make sure that you provide the training and one-on-one coaching team members need. Don't look at it as an extra cost; consider it a smart investment — one that opens up the opportunity of a limitless return.

ANNUAL SALES CHECKUP

THE SECRET TO SELLING SUCCESS boils down to how well salespeople execute the fundamentals — or "blocking and tackling," as one of my clients calls it. Even though there are many possible scapegoats for flat or declining sales, in the end, the true culprit is generally one or more missing fundamentals: the right talent, proper training, accountability or motivation.

Reinvigorate your sales efforts with this four-point sales checkup:

Checkpoint 1 — The Right Talent: Do you have the right talent in the right roles? Have you been asking farmers to hunt? Farmers prefer cultivating existing customer relationships. Hunters get energy from tracking down new opportunities. Training a farmer to hunt requires significant time and resources. If you're not sure how well team members fit their roles, consider having a formal assessment conducted.

Checkpoint 2 — Sales Skills: Does your sales team prepare enough for sales calls? How sharp are team members' conversational skills? When calling prospects, do they use a point of connection to build rapport, providing a compelling reason to meet? Do they listen actively? Do they conduct an effective needs assessment, identifying the prospect's pain points? Are they strong closers, keeping the ball in their court? Do they successfully overcome prospect objections? If you aren't sure, sit with them while they make their sales calls, or ride along to prospect meetings. After your assessment, develop an individualized training and coaching plan for each member of the team.

Checkpoint 3 — Accountability and Tracking: When you're confident you have the right people who are all properly trained, make sure you're holding them accountable for their performance. Boost success and reduce sales force frustration by focusing on sales activity, not just revenue numbers. While sales professionals can't control whether a prospect writes a check on schedule, they can control their own actions. If they're doing enough of the right activity and they have the proper skills, the sales will eventually follow. Once you're tracking the sales team's activity, you'll know if a particular member of the team is struggling. Remember that management has a responsibility to help inexperienced individuals. Let experienced veterans show off their sales skills during a live sales call, while their new teammate watches and learns.

Checkpoint 4 — Motivation and Attitude: Finally, take a look at each individual's attitude and level of motivation. Is your compensation plan encouraging the right behaviors? Are team members staying positive, or are they predicting negative outcomes before ever making calls?

Once you see the results of this four-point check, don't worry. Just remember that experienced sales trainers and coaches, whether internal or external, can get your sales team back in the winner's circle if you need a hand.

DELIVERING VALUE TO EDUCATED BUYERS

THESE DAYS, most buyers engage in significant online research before they ever consider speaking with sales professionals. Today's buyers are further along in the sales process, with a much clearer understanding of what they need, before your sales team ever says a word.

The good news is that new prospects are coming to the table more highly qualified than ever before, which helps your sales team become more efficient. However, because buyers have already done their homework, they have little patience for sales professionals who aren't complete experts in all of the details of their products and services, and how they stack up against the competition.

If you want to keep up, developing learning opportunities for your sales team is critical. Begin with intensive product training, including prospect drills where your sales team can practice handling tough customer questions and objections. Next, tackle more advanced sales skills, helping your team members understand their changing role in the sales process. Today's buyer is more sophisticated; they already know the features and benefits of your products or services. Instead, your team needs to learn to focus on consultative sales.

Today's educated buyer wants your sales team to be familiar with best practices, industry trends and creative uses for your products or services. If you're not sure that your sales team is currently adding value in this way, ask your newest customers. If they appreciated interacting with your sales team, you can rest easy, knowing that your team is offering intellectual value.

Make sure you supplement product and sales-skill training with knowledge about your competitors. Have your sales team shop competitors directly, reporting findings to the team. Your sales team has to understand how competitors are positioning themselves in the marketplace, especially compared to your company.

Because buyers can find anything online in just a few keystrokes, they crave immediate gratification. Your sales team needs to respond to needs quickly to avoid missing opportunities altogether. Set an aggressive response-time target, and then measure your sales and service teams against that metric to guarantee that you outperform your competitors.

You should also consider shifting from a geographical focus to vertical market focus. Today's consumers value expertise much more than physical proximity.

While your marketing effort can be fairly easily replicated by a motivated competitor, it is much more difficult to copy an effective sales team. Continue to invest in creating a solid sales culture with streamlined, efficient sales processes. It will set you miles ahead of your competitors.

NINE COMMON SALES TEAM HURDLES

DO YOU KNOW what's holding your sales team back? How can you guarantee consistent, exceptional performance? Usually, there are a handful of reasons why sales professionals aren't reaching their potential. Once your team clears these hurdles, you may be surprised how rapidly you see an improvement in performance.

Sales professionals often encounter non-buyers during the sales process. These individuals may influence the process, but they aren't the actual decision makers, so they can be significant time killers. One way around this hurdle is to start at the top of the house. The objective is to get a prompt and definitive answer from someone with the authority to accept or decline.

Low close ratios often signal a poor qualification process. Just getting more prospects in the sales pipeline isn't enough; make sure you've got the right prospects there.

Salespeople who want to work smarter instead of harder have always appreciated the difference that call preparation can make when it comes to landing new business. Those who skip this preparation are essentially rolling the dice like a telemarketer.

Systemize the sales process for your team by ensuring team members have the right tools. For example, you might invest in customer relationship management (CRM) software that integrates with their calendars. You might need up-to-date sales collateral or more plainspoken contracts. Relevant drip campaigns can also keep your brand name in front of prospects between conversations.

It's also important that your sales team builds a strong sense of value before discussing the price. If prospects see the value in the company's products or services, numbers are less likely to be a serious issue.

Persistence may be a virtue in sales, but it's just foolish to refuse to take no for an answer. When a salesperson gets a "no," encourage him to recognize that the prospect is giving him the freedom to move on to a prospect with a genuine interest, one that truly needs your products or services.

Encourage sales reps not to talk too much. A good rule of thumb is to listen 80 percent of the time, and talk only 20 percent of the time. Your sales team members should be aware of how much verbal space they're taking up in the conversation, giving prospects the opportunity to get a word in edgewise.

When a prospect says, "I'll think about it," teach your team not to let the prospect off the hook that easily. Gain insight into the reasons for the delay by saying, "Tell me more about your hesitation in moving forward." Peel back the layers until the the real objection is understood.

Remind your sales team members that they are in control of the situation. Even though prospects may be evaluating your products and services, your sales reps are evaluating them, too. If they aren't a good fit for your company, empower your team to walk away.

By clearing these hurdles, your sales team will be on the fast track to a record year.

THREE TIPS FOR IMPROVING A STRUGGLING SALES TEAM

SUCCESSFULLY MANAGING a sales team takes a special touch because great salespeople are just wired differently. Their fearlessness and dogged determination make them stellar at closing business — but these same qualities can also make them difficult to lead.

In addition to being high-energy, positive team players, the highest-performing sales professionals often have strong personalities. Occasionally, they can be impulsive and unrealistic. Good sales reps focus on solving problems and generating results, which is ultimately what you want them to do — but they don't necessarily feel the need to cross every "t" and dot every "i."

Fortunately, there is a three-part strategy you can adopt as a sales manager that will inspire your sales team to achieve even greater results.

Don't preach. Coach. When a member of your sales team has a skill gap, position yourself as coach instead of just telling the person what to do. Present the facts of the situation as a problem that needs to be solved, and then ask for the person's input — or even better, go on a few calls with your sales team to demonstrate how your strategy works. Once team members see your solution pay off, they will be eager to give it a shot.

Put away the rulebook. You need to track sales activity, of course, but beyond basic tracking, avoid creating complex sales processes that could end up tying the hands of your sales team. Find a balance between organization and micromanagement.

Celebrate successes. Most good "hunters" may be financially motivated, but that doesn't mean they are only motivated by dollar signs. Recognition from management, especially in front of their peers, still goes a long way. Beyond verbal recognition at sales meetings, consider small gift cards to their favorite dinner spots as a way of demonstrating that you know their preferences, an invitation to meet with a member of the senior management team, a paid Friday off, or even a high-potential lead hand-picked just for them. You might even consider shifting their least-liked task to another member of the team with a stronger affinity for that kind of work.

In the end, there's no single secret to success. No two sales people are alike, but if you understand what motivates each individual member of your team, you'll be able to bring out the best in all of them.

4

Only through introspection can we improve. Microsoft co-founder Bill Gates certainly understood this when he said, "I have been struck again and again by how important measurement is to improving the human condition." Thanks to technological advancements, our ability to easily measure sales and marketing strategies has improved exponentially. Gone are the days where it's good enough to simply monitor revenue growth and marketing expense, making vague correlations between the two. Today's savvy sales and marketing leaders make informed, data-driven decisions.

MEASURE YOUR SALES & MARKETING STRATEGIES

BENEFITS OF A DASHBOARD IN DRIVING COMPANY PERFORMANCE

NUMEROUS STUDIES SUPPORT the fact that companies which excel at aligning their marketing and sales efforts enjoy significantly higher revenue growth. A best-in-class strategy for creating such cohesion is the regular development of a business dashboard.

A dashboard is generally a one-page executive summary, often visual in nature, of the key metrics that drive your business. Data from a variety of sources is consolidated into a single, actionable report to allow all impacted stakeholders to quickly assess the state of the business and map out resulting next steps toward goal achievement.

There are various types of dashboards — from operational, to human resources, to customer service. The content of each is tailored for a particular point of view. With a customer service dashboard, for example, key drivers might include call volume, length of call, number of calls escalated, customer satisfaction scores and ultimately, repeat purchases.

Given that the goal of your sales and marketing effort is to drive incremental sales and profit, a growth dashboard — that focuses on the key drivers and indicators of growth within your business — is ideal for your sales and marketing team.

In determining the real success drivers for your outside sales team, consider: the number of referrals generated, the number of calls/meetings held with high-value targets, the length of the sales cycle, your team's close ratio, the cost of your team's time in closing sales, and the value of opportunities in the pipeline, all compared to comparable time periods as well as your targets.

From a marketing perspective, consider: the number of qualified inbound leads generated, the cost of acquisition for those inbound leads, improvements in market awareness of your brand, moving the needle on your online reputation, improvement in web-conversion rates, increases in online order size, and conversion from email subscriber to customer, as compared to previous quarter results and your goals.

All of that aside, the key to a successful dashboard effort has far less to do with how well the dashboard is built, and more to do with how regularly you share the data with your team, collectively assess its meaning, and calibrate your strategy accordingly.

Be sure to combine both sales and marketing drivers in the same dashboard, as both teams should ideally be working collectively toward the same targets. Conduct your review meetings with both teams in the same room to avoid finger pointing. For example, the sales team might convey that it would be more successful if the marketing team provided better leads.

To create a sustainable growth culture, one where you know that a defined level and type of activity will allow your company to realize its growth goals year after year, your sales and marketing teams must work in tandem, support one another, and be rewarded for teamwork that drives results.

PROJECTING SALES & MARKETING PLAN RETURNS

FAR TOO MANY COMPANIES look to past growth as the single best predictor of future growth in setting annual revenue targets with little analysis of the factors driving that past progress, anticipated market shifts over the coming year, and the predictability of the sales and marketing strategies built into their annual plans. It is a goal-setting process fraught with failure caused by either unrealistically high goals or those which aren't nearly aggressive enough.

Assuming you've measured prior year marketing efforts and assessed anticipated competitive and market factors, you are ready to develop a sales and marketing strategy — ideally one with predictable returns.

While plan predictability may sound like fortune telling, there's no hocus pocus to it. It's a science that begins with examination of returns on past sales and marketing efforts, as past measurement is what drives your ability to predict future results.

Not every sales and marketing strategy is easily measurable or predictable. The key is to "heavy up" your budget toward strategies that are, ensuring the returns generated by those measurable strategies more than cover your entire plan budget.

Digital strategies, such as search engine pay-per-click campaigns, are highly measurable. Set up properly, you can easily gauge a consumer's conversion to a sale after entering your targeted keywords into a search engine and ultimately clicking on your sponsored campaign.

Let's say that last year, you had a $50K search engine pay-per-click campaign budget. For simplicity sake, let's assume you invested half in keyword combination A and half in keyword combination B. Combo A generated a 2 to 1 return, turning $25K into $50K, with combo B generating a 4 to 1 return, generating $100K from that same $25K return. All in, you earned $150K from a $50K return.

Now this year, you opt to put the full $50K into combo B that you can predict, assuming all other marketplace factors are even, will generate $200K in returns. Now naturally, all marketplace factors are never even, and their anticipated impact on your returns must be accounted for.

Generally speaking, look at your sales and marketing plan investment in two buckets — proven and unproven. Put about 80 percent of your budget into strategies with a history for proven pay off and 20 percent into testing new, innovative strategies for possible larger-scale deployment in future years or those tactics that you know you must deploy but cannot be easily measured.

With more and more companies feeling pressure to deliver a return on their sales and marketing investments, and increasing technological advancements allowing sales and marketing professionals to do just that, say goodbye to hope-based goal setting. Demonstrate your value as a cutting-edge marketing or sales professional by demonstrating the predictability of your plan.

SALES MEASUREMENT TECHNIQUES TO MOVE THE NEEDLE

UNLESS YOU HAVE MORE SALES from ideal customers than you know what to do with, your organization can benefit from sales measurement strategies. They allow you to not only forecast future sales but also to dissect your team's success through each step of the sales cycle in order to fine-tune your approach and improve results.

Often, determination of your sales metrics results in adjustments to the way you are tracking your sales activities, ultimately allowing you to capture more meaningful, actionable data.

When discerning the sales metrics most relevant in your industry and most likely to move the needle within your specific company, begin internally and then look externally.

Internal Vantage Point: Examine your employee satisfaction and retention rates as the most basic indicators of strong company performance.

Next up, examine your entire sales process. Begin with the length of your sales cycle overall, and ideally monitor it each step along the way. If you operate an accounting firm, for example, you might assess how long it takes to: qualify a prospect in or out, land an initial first meeting, develop a proposal, get that proposal delivered, and help the prospect reach a decision.

Then, assess how many active high-value prospects there are at each step in your process, the value of opportunities in your pipeline overall, and the cost of your team's time in closing sales.

External Vantage Point: Track your customer retention, as countless studies support how markedly less expensive it is to retain a client versus attract a new one. Monitor annual customer spend and satisfaction as gauges of basic loyalty, as well as referrals generated by existing customers as the ultimate litmus test for even higher loyalty levels.

Consider hiring a research firm to survey your current and past customers to ask them how you stack up against your competitors and what percentage of category spend your firm is receiving versus your competition.

Survey prospects and the broader marketplace to determine how your brand stacks up against competitors on each of your key differentiators and what's preventing prospects from doing business with you. Price shop your competitors and be sure to include your rates and theirs on your dashboard. If you are in a B2C (business to consumer) industry, consider including customer sentiments reflected via third-party review and social-media sites; there are numerous web-based tools which can provide these metrics.

Incorporate selected metrics into the overall growth dashboard for your firm and review it regularly, compared to prior time periods, with your sales and marketing teams collectively. Be nimble and prepared to flex your strategy based on the findings.

THE PRIORITIES OF THE DATA-DRIVEN MARKETER

WHEN I BEGAN MY CAREER in marketing more than 20 years ago, measurement was straightforward. We simply monitored revenue growth and our marketing expense, making assumptions about how the two might be correlated. Sure, there was a bit of basic offer tracking, and we certainly looked at total impressions, but for the lion's share of marketing activities, meaningful data just wasn't available.

In contrast, today's marketer is profoundly data-driven. In fact, there is so much potential data to monitor that the task can be arduous. Avoid getting overwhelmed by focusing on these specific marketing-measurement priorities, from DOMO's "7 Secrets of the Data-Driven CMO."

Manage by exception. It is impossible to stay abreast of and act on every bit of data available to you. Instead, manage by exception by focusing on data that differs significantly from what you planned — either above or below the projection. Take a deep dive to figure out why.

Measure the "unmeasurables." It's easy to say that branding and buyer attitudes about your brand aren't measurable, but the truth is that they just aren't easily measurable. It can be done. If surveying the market isn't a practical measurement technique, look instead at growth in social-media brand mentions, growth in direct visits to your website, where your URL was intentionally keyed, as well as growth in the number of brand-related search terms used.

Test everything. Every conceivable strategy possible should be tested, if you have the resources to do so. If it performs well in tests, keep it and continue to test it to fine tune the strategy. If it doesn't test well, kill it. Move on to another strategy.

A/B testing, also called split testing, is where you compare two versions of a web page with only one variable that's different — such as a headline — to see which one performs better. It works equally well with email campaigns (subject line testing) and social media content (two versions of a Facebook ad featuring different designs).

Benchmark conversion rates. A conversion is defined as the number of site visitors or email recipients, for example, that end up becoming paying customers. Knowing your past conversion rates allows you to identify upticks that can later be repeated. It's also essential to know standard industry benchmarks so that you have an external form of comparison, versus just likening to your own past performance.

With a bevy of marketing metrics at your disposable, staying focused on what matters most will ensure you have the capacity to actually take action on what is most likely to impact the overall performance of your marketing strategy, instead of getting buried in the weeds.